HACHIJO
ISLE OF EXILE

Hachijo: ISLE OF EXILE

photographs by TSUNE SUGIMURA
text by SHIGEO KASAI

WEATHERHILL
New York • Tokyo

The photographs in this book have also appeared in *Hachijo-jima: Runin To no Fudo to Ningen* (Hachijo Island: Customs and People of the Exile Island), published by Kodansha, Tokyo. The text, translated, reorganized, and adapted for Western readers by Ronald V. Bell, Akito Miyamoto, and Albert Brewster, is based on materials chiefly drawn from *Hachijo-jima Runin Meimei Den* (Brief Lives of Hachijo Island Exiles) by Shigeo Kasai and Kanzo Yoshida, published by Yoshida Nankoen, Tokyo.

FIRST EDITION, 1973

Published by John Weatherhill, Inc., 149 Madison Avenue, New York, N.Y. 10016, with editorial offices at 7-6-13 Roppongi, Minato-ku, Tokyo 106. Photographs copyright © 1972 by Tsune Sugimura. Text copyright © 1973 by Shigeo Kasai; all rights reserved. Printed in Japan.

Library of Congress Cataloging in Publication Data: Kasai, Shigeo, 1916– / Hachijo: isle of exile. / The photos have also appeared in Hachijo-jima: runin to no fudo to ningen. The text, translated, reorganized and adapted for Western readers by Ronald V. Bell, Akito Miyamoto, and Albert Brewster, is based on materials chiefly drawn from Hachijo-jima: runin meimei den. / 1. Hachijō (Island)— History. / 2. Hachijō (Island)—Exiles. / I. Sugimura, Tsune, 1926– illus. / DS895.H3K37 / 952'.135 / 72-92258 / ISBN 0-8348-0081-0

CONTENTS

HACHIJO
ISLE OF EXILE

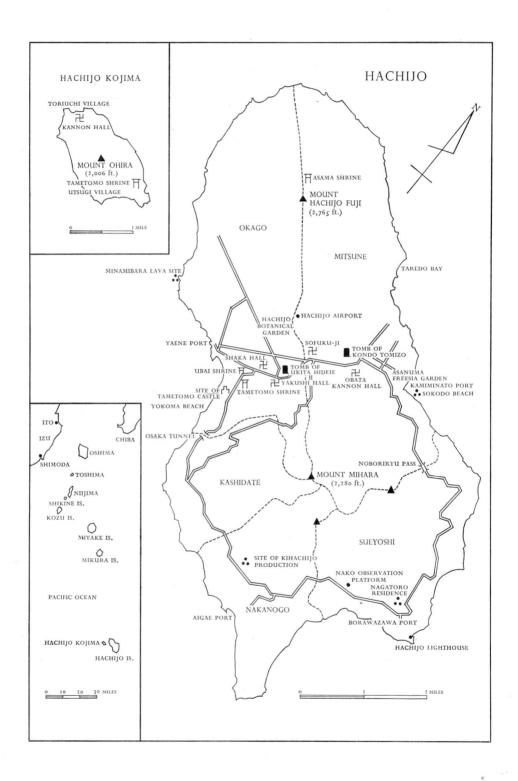

HACHIJO KOJIMA

TORIUCHI VILLAGE
卍
KANNON HALL

▲ MOUNT OHIRA
(2,006 ft.)
TAMETOMO SHRINE 卍
UTSUGI VILLAGE

0   1 MILE

HACHIJO

N

卍 ASAMA SHRINE

▲ MOUNT
HACHIJO FUJI
(2,765 ft.)

OKAGO

MITSUNE

TAREDO BAY

MINAMIBARA LAVA SITE

HACHIJO
BOTANICAL
GARDEN

● HACHIJO AIRPORT

SOFUKU-JI
卍

YAENE PORT

SHAKA HALL
卍

TOMB OF
KONDO TOMIZO

UBAI SHRINE
卍

TOMB OF
UKITA HIDEIE

ASANUMA
FREESIA GARDEN

YAKUSHI HALL
卍

OBATA
KANNON HALL

KAMIMINATO PORT
● SOKODO BEACH

SITE OF
TAMETOMO CASTLE
YOKOMA BEACH

TAMETOMO SHRINE
卍

OSAKA TUNNEL

ITO ●

IZU

CHIBA

OSHIMA

SHIMODA ●

● TOSHIMA

NIIJIMA

SHIKINE IS.

KOZU IS.

MIYAKE IS.

MIKURA IS.

PACIFIC OCEAN

HACHIJO KOJIMA ○

HACHIJO IS.

0   10   20   30 MILES

KASHIDATE

NOBORIRYU PASS

▲ MOUNT MIHARA
(2,280 ft.)
▲

SUEYOSHI

SITE OF KIHACHIJO
PRODUCTION

NAKO OBSERVATION
PLATFORM
NAGATORO
RESIDENCE

AIGAE PORT

NAKANOGO

BORAWAZAWA PORT

HACHIJO LIGHTHOUSE

0   1   2 MILES

I PUNISHMENT, LAW, AND THE JAPANESE

EXILE IS AS OLD as the gods. Witness, in Japanese mythology, the banishment from the land of the gods of the windstorm deity Susa-no-wo and, in the Bible, the casting out of heaven of Lucifer and, later, Adam and Eve. The logic behind it is that if for one reason or another a dangerous troublemaker cannot be executed or incarcerated out of reach of his friends, then banishment from the seat of power is the next best means for ending or curtailing his influence.

The *Kojiki* (Record of Ancient Matters; A.D. 712) gives the earliest mention of the practice of banishment in Japan. An aggressive troublemaker, Susa-no-wo was delegated by his father Izanagi to rule the ocean. Unlike his obedient brother and sister, he betrayed his father's trust by remaining in the land of the gods, where he raised a great din. He wept and howled so mightily that the mountains withered and the rivers and seas dried up. His father's anger turned to boiling rage when Susa-no-wo told him that instead of taking charge of tides and currents and sea life he wanted to visit the land of his mother. With that Izanagi expelled him "with a divine expulsion." Izanagi is soon dropped from the *Kojiki* narrative, but Susa-no-wo goes on to further troublemaking that earns him a second divine expulsion, this one at the command of the council of the gods.

Before the introduction of Buddhism, in the middle of the sixth century A.D., prisoners convicted of serious crimes were more likely to be punished by execution than banishment. According to a Chinese document of the third century, the punishment for grave offenses was extermination of the offender, his household, and his kinsmen. One of the first recorded instances of a punishment tells of the tattooing in A.D. 400 of a nobleman named Azumi Hamako for conspiring against Emperor Richu. An imperial princess, Karu no Oiratsune, holds the dubious distinction of being the first Japanese exile on record. She was banished by her father, Emperor Ingyo, in A.D. 435. Places of confinement probably existed from a very early time, but the earliest mention of one does not occur until 483

9

when, we are told, Emperor Seinei made a personal inspection of a jail. A Chinese history, written about 630, says that banishment and flogging were common forms of punishment in sixth-century Japan, as was execution for murder, arson, and adultery. The *Omi Ryo,* the first systematic code of Japanese laws and ordinances, was compiled by Fujiwara no Kamatari and promulgated by Emperor Tenji in 668. This code, which was amended several times, formed the basis of the Taiho Code, a ten-volume compilation of laws.

The Taiho Code outlines the punishments to be applied to criminals as capital punishment (beheading or strangulation), banishment (nearby, middle distant, far), imprisonment with labor (from one to three years), flogging with a stick (from sixty to one hundred blows), and whipping (from ten to fifty blows). Examination of a prisoner by torture was also used when he would not confess.

During the reign of Empress Koken (749–58) a Shinto priest and priestess who had stood high in imperial favor were merely banished for conspiring against the throne. And several hundred persons who commited the same crime in 757 had sentences of death commuted to banishment because of the prayers of a Buddhist nun who was of the imperial lineage.

The strictures against execution were not always observed by Koken and her courtiers. Although she abdicated in 758, she retained power, advised by a Rasputin-like monk named Dokyo. And when a supporter of the emperor failed in a revolt against her, she had the emperor demoted to the rank of prince and banished to the Inland Sea island of Awaji where, not long after, he was strangled. Koken reassumed the throne, this time with the name Shotoku, and raised her monk-lover to the rank of chancellor-priest, a position just below that of the throne itself. But Dokyo was ambitious for even more; he wanted the throne itself. His attempt to get it was foiled by a courtier who reported that the oracle of the gods at Usa had declared that Dokyo was ineligible for the throne because he was not of imperial lineage. Dokyo was able to have the messenger degraded and banished for bringing back a false report, but with the death of Koken shortly afterward his influence declined rapidly and he in turn was banished from the capital, never again to wield power.

From 818 to 1156, chiefly under the influence of Buddhism, the death penalty was officially prohibited and banishment, which had been ranked next in severity as punishment for political crimes, became the maximum punishment. Abolishing the death penalty did not mean the end of severe reprisals against lawbreakers. A person convicted of robbery, for example, was liable to have his arm chopped off, which suggests the simple concepts of social retribution that prevailed.

It was not only Buddhist injunctions against taking life that favored banishment over a sentence of death; superstition was rife in the society of the time and even the rulers believed that the ghost of a murdered or executed person roamed the earth seeking vengeance. The force of this belief was so great that the emperor Kammu, who had moved the court in 784 from Nara to Nagaoka, issued in 793 a new edict that directed that work be stopped at the new site and preparations be made for another move, this time to nearby Heian (present Kyoto). The move, which was achieved at tremendous cost, was made to escape the vengeful spirit of the emperor's younger brother who had been sent into exile and allowed to starve to death there for his part in a murder and conspiracy.

The goals of banishment could be achieved by methods more subtle but just as effective as open punishment for crime. One such method was to post an out-of-favor official to a province far from the capital. This is what happened to Sugawara Michizane (845–903). An accomplished statesman, poet, and calligrapher of the Heian period, his meteoric rise to the second highest office in the land brought him the envy of the powerful Fujiwara family. Although Michizane stood high in the favor of the retired emperor, the Fujiwaras were able to pressure the new sovereign into appointing him supernumerary viceroy of Kyushu. In Heian times to be a mere twenty miles from the capital was to be effectively cut off from the source of national power. To Michizane, distant Kyushu must have seemed as remote as the stars. The emperor never gained the power necessary to recall him and Michizane, yearning for the delights of the capital, died in exile.

On the eve of his departure into exile he addressed this poem to the plum tree in his garden:

> When the east wind blows,
> Send me your fragrance
> And forget not the spring,
> Though I am gone,
> O blossom of the plum.

Men who fell from high favor sometimes found it necessary to sever their connections at court and go into temporary exile. In this way they could put themselves beyond the reach of powerful enemies while easing pressures on patrons and friends. Murasaki Shikibu, who, as an attendant of Empress Shoshi, was herself familiar with the practices and intrigues of Heian court life, has Prince Genji, the hero of her novel *The Tale of Genji*, exile himself to Suma when "the intrigue against him was becoming every day more formidable." Her account reveals the frustration and loneliness that troubled exiles from the Heian court. Genji fears most of all that his exile may become permanent and that he may not be able to care for the well-being of his loved ones.

A certain measure of disgrace inevitably clung to the exile and his family. Genji remarks at one point that people whom the government disapproves of are expected to creep about miserably in the dark, and if they try to make themselves happy and comfortable, it is considered very wicked. His own departure from the capital is a quiet one, marked with the show of humility expected of people in disgrace.

The weak do well not to try the patience of powerful enemies, and no doubt most exiles made their departure as inconspicuous as possible. At rare times, however, the balance of power lay in doubt and the departing exile, though not strong enough to defy the ruler, could afford to flaunt his disrespect. The *Taiheiki,* a feudal-period chronicle, describes the banishment in the mid-fourteenth century of the retainers of a man named Sasaki who had torn branches from the cloistered emperor's maple trees, fought with the men sent to stop them, and finally tried to burn down the cloistered emperor's palace. The shogun ordered the arsonists out of Kyoto, but such was the power situation that they defied convention by dressing themselves in gorgeous clothes and, mounted on caparisoned steeds, rode merrily away, each carrying a caged nightingale.

Another form of exile that did not go by the name was the practice of forced abdication. The office of emperor or shogun could be so trying, so fraught with burdensome ceremony or exposed to danger that abdication was not at all uncommon nor always unwelcome. In 1300, to cite an unusual example, five ex-emperors were living. Since the men who held these offices were commonly mere figureheads, it often happened that they were forced to abdicate by the men who held the real power. Sometimes, in fact, the real power behind the throne was an abdicated emperor or empress: we have already seen how the ex-empress Koken was able to force the emperor to vacate the throne. And while the emperor was the symbol of unity around which great armies could be rallied, it was usually not he who controlled the fighting men but the men who used his office and controlled him. A complaisant emperor would be allowed to occupy the throne, performing the ceremonial functions required of him and enjoying the pleasures of a highly refined court. One who resisted too much would be forced to abdicate, and if he refused, it was not unlikely that he would be assassinated. Usually, however, the threat of assassination was enough to convince a reluctant emperor to step down. Not all ex-emperors had to leave the capital, although in many cases it was judged prudent to retire to a secluded retreat. There a man could live a meditative or a pleasure-seeking life, at a safe remove from the intrigues that could cost him his life.

The end of the Heian period (1185) was marked by the rise of the military clans. Not surprisingly, the battle-toughened warriors who ruled Japan during the next several hundred years were far less fastidious about taking human life than had been the courtlier rulers of Nara and Heian Japan. Although banishment was still practiced, meting out summary justice for high crimes was more in keeping with the warriors' inclination for direct action. Headless troublemakers, they knew, no longer made trouble.

Convicted clergy, however, because of their holy office, were often able to escape the death penalty. Instead they suffered banishment, usually to an inhospitable area where, it was hoped, they would perish by "natural" causes. An exception was made in the case of warrior-monks, the so-called *sohei*. When they opposed the sixteenth-century warlord Oda Nobunaga, he had them slaughtered by the tens of thousands and their monasteries gutted. But while Nobunaga had lay followers of the disputatious Nichiren sect executed after they caused disorders at Kyoto in 1536, he merely banished the priests of the sect. Even Nobunaga, the cruelest of the cruel leaders of these times, was occasionally moved to spare clergy from execution.

Nichiren (1222–82), the head of the sect that bears his name, himself had been banished from Kamakura, headquarters of the military government from 1261 to 1263, for admonishing the rulers. When he returned to the capital, the headstrong evangelist was unchanged and he began to berate the authorities more furiously than ever. In 1271 the authorities lost all patience with the extraordinarily dissident monk and arranged to have him secretly executed. But just as the soldier who was to behead him raised his sword, one account goes, a ball of light came from the direction of Enoshima and blinded the executioner so that he fell to the ground quivering with fright. Whether by divine intervention, lightning, or some other natural phenomenon, Nichiren was saved. But he was too troublesome to be allowed near the capital and he was sent into exile again, this time to Sado, a remote island off the Japan Sea coast.

Although it was not until the seventeenth century that Hachijo Island was first used as a place of banishment, other islands of the Seven Islands of Izu (of which Hachijo is one) were used from an early date. The most famous of the Seven Islands' early exiles was Minamoto no Tametomo, a warrior who was banished to Oshima Island after his defeat in the Hogen War in 1156. Exile, however, did not prove confining to Tametomo. Soon after his arrival on Oshima, he raised a small army, placed them in boats, and set out to conquer the Seven Islands. He accomplished this and went on to fight and win more battles on the mainland against the Taira clan, his family's traditional enemy, but was at last unsuccessful. Many legends and tales have been told about Tametomo's heroic exploits (some of which will be recounted later in this narrative). The most famous of these says that when, in 1170, he saw the fleet of his enemies coming to attack him, he took an arrow and aimed it at the boat of the Taira leader. The arrow struck with such force that it pierced the hull and foundered the boat. Having accomplished that deed, Tametomo rode home and there committed harakiri, ritual disembowelment. It is an ironic footnote to history that Tametomo, an exile himself, was the first conquerer of Hachijo.

2 THE ISLAND IN THE BLACK TIDE

HACHIJO ISLAND DID not become a penal colony until 1606, when the Tokugawa military government, the shogunate, sent Ukita Hideie and thirteen members of his family there. Islands, of course, because of their surrounding seas, are natural places of banishment, and Hachijo, because of its remoteness from the new military capital in Edo (the present Tokyo), was adjudged a good place for confining actual or potential troublemakers. The island served the authorities well. During its 275 years as a penal colony it held a total of 1900 exiles, of whom only a very small number are believed to have escaped to the mainland.

Hachijo's forty-some-odd square miles have been formed by nature in the shape of a squat sakè decanter with its narrow mouth pointing toward the northwest as though thrown by a drunk and dissatisfied customer at the semicircular bar that is the mainland of Japan. At the island's western end is Mount Hachijo Fuji, a dormant volcano that rises in gentle curves to a single-humped summit 2,765 feet above the treacherous currents of the Kuro Shio, the Black Tide. Near the eastern end, like a counterweight to Hachijo Fuji, squats Mount Mihara, a 2,280-foot extinct volcano. Hachijo Fuji has not erupted for about 265 years and has grown a dense green coverlet of vegetation.

During squalls, when the island is being drenched in one place while steaming in the sunlight a few yards away, the maritime nature of the island is revealed. Typhoons annually sweep up from the south in late summer and early autumn, drenching the island in a fury of wind and water. Typhoons are a fearsome but accepted aspect of island life. And during much of the rest of the year the island is a windy place with air currents so strong that islanders refer to winds of sixty or seventy feet per minute as light airs.

The climate is warm and humid; it is so wet that the island registers the second highest rainfall in Japan. It is an ideal agricultural climate. Almost all of Hachijo is covered with broad-leaf evergreens and new growth springs up with jungle-like rapidity. Within six or seven years after a tree has been cut down, it grows back into fine firewood and charcoal sources.

Most of Japan's small islands suffer from a shortage of water, but Hachijo is an exception. Water is plentiful there, and due to its water resources Hachijo has had a long history of rice cultivation, long but of limited acreage. If it had not been for its rice the island would most likely have experienced far worse famines than it did. All in all, from a geographical and climatic standpoint, the exiles banished from Edo to Hachijo might have been sent to far worse places. Certainly convicts sent to Sado Island, a damp chilly hellhole where they were made to labor underground in government mines, were far worse off. But however better than Sado it was, Hachijo too was a hell on earth to the criminals sent there.

The first exiles sent to Hachijo were political prisoners, people who had held high places in the social scale of the feudal period. For the seventy years that Ukita Hideie and his family lived in banishment on Hachijo, relatively few other exiles were sent there and these only at irregular intervals. Like Hideie, most of the exiles sent to the island in the seventeenth century were being punished for political or ideological crimes or for belonging to a proscribed religious group, such as the Fuju Fuse sect of Nichiren Buddhism. Far from being hardened or incorrigible criminals most were persons of culture, intellectuals or in some other capacity people of quality. It is not surprising then that the attitude of the islanders toward them was one of respect and admiration rather than fear and scorn.

Once on the island, exiles were permitted a great deal of freedom and because of their status the islanders did not treat them as criminals but instead welcomed them as bringers of new knowledge. In time the islanders began to refer to them as *kunnu,* a respectful term meaning "mainlanders," and to invite them to their homes. It was at gatherings like these that the exiles taught the islanders the popular songs and dances of Edo. Even today old festival songs reminiscent of those sung on the mainland can be heard. One of these, which suggests the way that at least some of the exiles came to feel about the island, says:

> Hachijo Island, from the ocean
> It seems an ogre's lair,
> But once on its shores
> You learn it's an island of love.

The love that the song refers to is perhaps the attachment that developed between the exiles and their island mistresses. These were women refered to as *mizukumi-onna,* or water-drawing women. Although exiles were allowed to bring

A

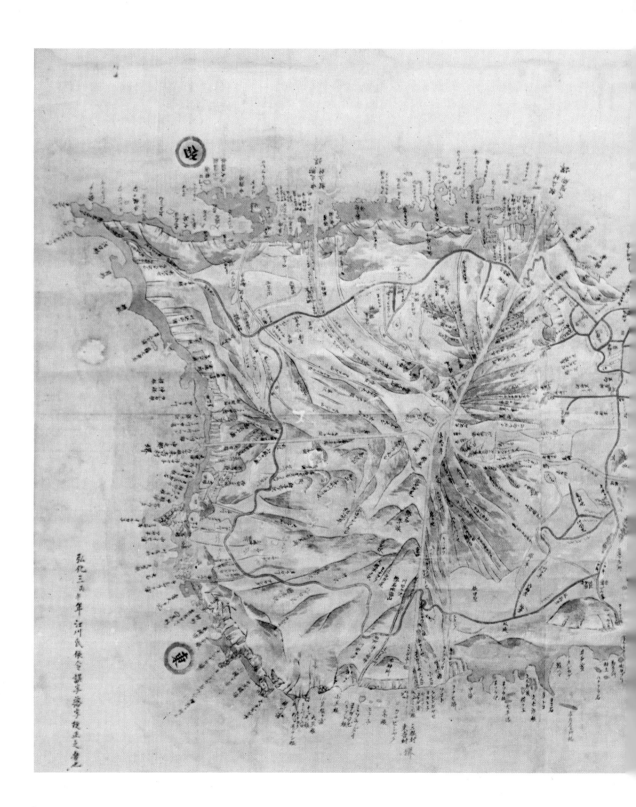

B

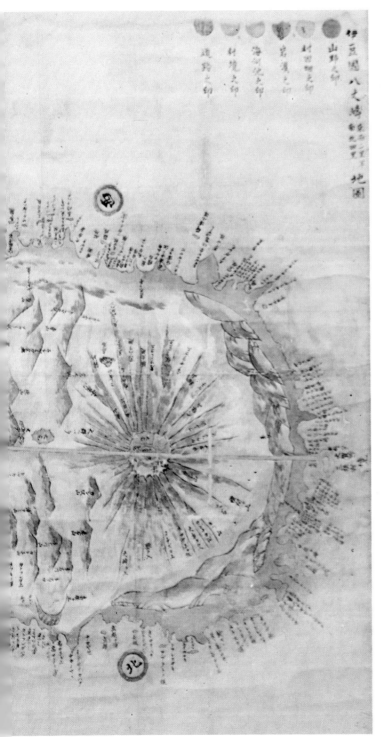

C

D

E

F

G

H   J

I

4

8

15

their children with them to the island, their wives were prohibited from accompanying them. Even Ukita Hideie, the highest ranking exile ever detained at Hachijo, was forced to leave his wife on the mainland. The island has traditionally had a larger population of women than men, so that the difficulty of finding husbands, along with the loneliness of the exiles, naturally brought these men and women together.

The exiles were given small homes soon after their arrival in the village to which they were assigned, and home ownership forced them into doing the unfamiliar chores of housekeeping. When the young women of the island saw the exiles attempting to adjust to these unfamiliar circumstances, sympathy led them to help out with such tasks as drawing water, sewing clothes, and preparing meals. Circumstances like these led to firm and intimate attachments, and mutual housekeeping and the birth of children followed as matters of course.

The men of the island tolerated these arrangements. No doubt, too, because of the surplus of women and the respectful status of the early exiles, parents often encouraged the unions. Until the Meiji era, which began in 1868, most of the exiles "married" a *mizukumi-onna*. Legally these unions were not binding, but the tolerant islanders did not make social distinctions between exiles' wives and islanders' wives. When an exile was pardoned, if he wished, he was allowed to take his wife and children with him. Some, like the sculptor Mimbu, did of course; others already had wives and children on the mainland, and many of these men left their island wives behind. Although no mention is made in the old records, the relations between a married exile and an island woman were no doubt deeply marked in measure to his chances of pardon.

Far more than for a man, the situation for a woman was potentially tragic. Her horizons always held the fear that with the granting of a pardon to her mate, she would be left as bereft as a widow. Even worse, the pardoned exile might decide to take only his children with him. By law he could, and no doubt some men did.

In 1777, during a period of severe famine, the authorities promulgated a law prohibiting conjugal arrangements between exiles and islanders. They gave as their reason the shortage of food on the island, pointing to the fact that the children resulting from these unions worsened an already dangerous situation: more mouths required more food, and there was precious little of that. It was simple arithmetic. But even so the authorities, at least those on the island, must have known that as long as food enough for the present and a little beyond that was available, a more intense calculus would prevail. The prohibition was ineffective; after all, what official could take the time and trouble to spy out clandestine romance, for that is certainly what would happen if the law had to be enforced. When real food shortages threatened, there was even less time for such petty enforcement because even the law enforcement officials had to devote themselves almost wholly to food gathering.

Surprisingly, few cases of violent behavior occurred on Hachijo. This was true even after the quality of the prisoners changed from cultured men to ordinary criminals. The chief reason for the good behavior of the exiles is the treatment they received from the islanders, especially the *mizukumi-onna*. Had exiles and islanders been forcefully kept apart, the situation would certainly have been different. Even though the exiles were almost wholly cut off from contact with family and friends on the mainland, their loneliness and frustration were soothed by the compassionate Hachijo women. This is another reason why the proscription against exile-*mizukumi-onna* arrangements failed. Since the officials were charged with keeping public order—and Tokugawa officialdom was characterized by an at times fanatical passion for keeping order in the most trivial matters—it was in their interest to overlook minor offenses that promoted peaceful social relations. Even the most feeble-minded, officious, petty bureaucrat could understand that much.

An incident that occurred in 1860, shows clearly where the loyalty of the *mizukumi-onna* lay. A group of thirty exiles, led by a man named Ryuemon, planned to escape from the island. Through their own carelessness, they were found out and captured. Most of them paid with their lives for the attempt. Although the *mizukumi-onna* knew of the escape plans, not one of them leaked word to the officials or the other islanders. They kept the secret well, and some of them even helped in the preparations. The seven that did help out were convicted and punished. This incident, in which two islanders and another exile were killed by the rioting exiles was the most violent in the island's history. But this is a story we will come to later.

3 UKITA HIDEIE: THE UNVANQUISHED WARRIOR

UKITA HIDEIE, THE first exile sent to Hachijo, had been the daimyo, or feudal lord, of Mimasaka Province, the area that is now Okayama Prefecture. He had also been one of the Five Great Elders (*Go Tairo*), the most powerful group in Japan in the last decade of the sixteenth century. His father died when Hideie was a child and he was raised by Toyotomi Hideyoshi, the military dictator who ruled Japan at this time. When Hideyoshi died in 1598, the uneasy peace he had brought soon began to disintegrate. In the struggles between the great warlords that followed, Hideie allied himself with the losing faction, the lords who pitted themselves against Tokugawa Ieyasu, the strongest and most capable of them all. In 1600, at the Battle of Sekigahara, Ieyasu's army defeated those of Hideie and his allies. Hideie fled south to Satsuma Province in Kyushu and was deprived of his fief. From Satsuma in 1603, he went north, to Suruga, and there he stayed in hiding until 1605, when he was taken into custody by Tokugawa officials and condemned to death.

Although defeated, Hideie was not without influence. His wife was a member of the powerful Maeda family and he himself was a friend of Shimazu, lord of Satsuma Province. When Shimazu and the Maedas pleaded Hideie's cause, Ieyasu reduced his sentence to perpetual exile on Hachijo, at the same time stripping him of all rank and emoluments. He was thirty-four at the time.

In Hideyoshi's invasion of Korea in 1592, Hideie had been a twenty-year-old commander in chief. At thirty-four his public career was finished. But this remarkable man lived until 1655, when a mortal illness finally brought to an end his half-century of exile.

In keeping with the high rank he had held, and the influential supporters he still had, the treatment given Hideie and his family while at Hachijo far surpassed that given any of the exiles who followed. Every other year, until 1869, when his descendants were granted amnesty, the Maedas sent Hideie's family seventy bales

67

of polished rice, together with clothing, medicine, gold coins in the amount of thirty-five *ryo,* and other supplies.

It is not recorded whether Hideie had a *mizukumi-onna.* His son Hidetaka, who had accompanied him into exile (along with twelve other persons, including another son, servants, a nurse to care for the boys, and a physician), did. He was permitted to marry one of the deputy-magistrate's daughters. If Hideie did take an island wife, she probably did not bear him any children, for there is no record of any such child, and if one had been born it would have been extremely difficult to hide. In any case, the family expanded greatly and when a pardon was granted two hundred and sixty-four years after Hideie first landed on the island, there were twenty Ukita families. Today many of Hideie's descendants still live on Hachijo, although they write the family name with different characters from those he used.

Either the family grew with extraordinary rapidity or the Ukitas, unused to reduced circumstances, were unable to live within their budget. An undated account tells us of a meal the former commander in chief was once invited to share with a visiting deputy magistrate from Edo. One of the dishes served contained three balls of rice. Hideie ate one ball and wrapped the other two in paper to take home to his family. This so moved the magistrate that he granted him a bale of rice. Perhaps Hideie's behavior was only a display of soldierly frugality, but whatever the reason, the plummet from the ranks of the Five Great Elders to penurious-seeming exile was a long, long fall.

It would be interesting to know what Hideie thought of during his exile, whether he regretted his decision to oppose Tokugawa Ieyasu, whether he was bitter against the people who imprisoned him or grateful because they had not executed him. And why did he choose the disgrace of demotion and banishment rather than the honorable way offered by ritual disembowelment? But there is no such record; Hideie seems to have been tight-lipped in the extreme. One source suggests that he slipped into an untroubled life of fishing and occasional poetry writing because he did not want to cause difficulties for the Shimazu clan. The absence of any record of his thoughts during exile makes it tempting to speculate.

Earlier we mentioned the not uncommon practice of abdication by Japanese emperors and shoguns. And a theme that runs through accounts of the lives of ranking men and women is the desire to escape from the punishing demands of public life to some quiet retreat at a temple or villa some distance from the city. Taking the tonsure, a gesture meant to signify retreat from mundane affairs and ambitions, was a common means of escape. Officials were also known to drop out by putting their affairs in order and resigning from all official positions. Among the reasons for such resignation might be the death of a loved one, a sharp setback to ambitious undertaking, the betrayal of a friend, or any of a number of the things that can make a man stop in full stride and reconsider his goals and perhaps decide that all ambition really is vanity. The emphasis that Buddhism places on resignation plays a part here too. So it may well be that the man whose brilliant rise to twenty-year-old commander in chief of an army of over a hundred thousand men, to the ranks of the five most powerful men in the country, and who almost surely entertained thoughts of being the most powerful man in the country, after the betrayal and defeat at Sekigahara, decided that the price was not worthy of the effort, the goals illusory.

Perhaps too he saw his exile as a symbol of unswerving loyalty to the cause he had fought for at Sekigahara. The great betrayals he and his allies suffered there may have convinced him that he alone of the leaders of the time had endured with his integrity unsoiled. A brief anecdote from this period suggests that this may be so.

A few years after he was sent into exile, a messenger came in secret to deliver a proposal from the Maedas. They offered to intercede with the Tokugawas to secure a position for him as lord of a province. He was not to expect too much, but they thought they might get him a small province. The messenger arrived at mealtime. Hideie heard the man out, carefully laid down his chopsticks, and said simply, "I was one of the Five Elders of the Toyotomi family. I have no desire to establish any relations with the Tokugawas. I appreciate the Maedas' efforts on my behalf, but I must decline." Perhaps the Maedas might not have been able to secure his release, but with these proud, unyielding words Hideie perpetuated his banishment.

4 THE EXILE LIFE

BEGINNING IN 1704, the quality of Hachijo's exiles underwent a major change. The laws of the time were exacting to an inordinate degree and, human nature being what it is, common criminals were in no short supply in the capital. Robbers and pickpockets, vengeance killers and unpremeditated murderers, incendiaries and passionate firebugs, rapists and adulterers, intimidators and petty thieves, mayhem specialists and run-of-the-mill street brawlers, top-class courtesans and pushover whores, high-livers and low-living gutter vagabonds, erring priests and prodigal sons gone the whole route, and all the fall guys and fall girls who get in the way of powerful people—all these and more found themselves contemplating the receeding shore as the prison boat bound for Hachijo headed out of Tokyo Bay.

Before 1742 crimes punishable by banishment were not spelled out in law, the punishment of a condemned person being left to the somewhat arbitrarily arrived at decision of the magistrate in charge of the case. In that year, however, a code of one hundred articles was compiled in which crimes deserving exile were specified. Among these were murder, arson, gambling, and seriously injuring or crippling a person. Members of outlawed religions were also singled out for banishment. There were at this time two religious sects, the Fuju Fuse and the Mishima, that the government had proscribed, and people who preached their doctrines, sheltered their preachers, or who belonged to the sects and refused to convert, were to be exiled. Christianity was also proscribed, but by the eighteenth century most Japanese Christians had either been executed, had apostatized, or gone into hiding.

Sex crimes are also mentioned in the law. Curiously though, the specification that banishment be the penalty for raping or injuring a female juvenile was repealed in the following year. Not only were the authorities interested in a monk's doctrines but they also regulated his sex life, threatening him with banishment if he committed adultery.

Although the sword was revered to the point of idolatry by the warrior class (it was endowed by many swordsmen with a spirit), the firearm, since its introduction into Japan in 1542, had drawn increasing if grudging respect. The sword would be revered and wielded by any aspiring rebel leader but he knew full well that in the end it would be guns that would decide an issue of arms. The authorities, naturally, were also well aware of the efficacy of firearms and they took great pains to control possession of them. Guards at the barriers on the roads leading into the capital were under strict orders to watch out for persons trying to smuggle weapons into Edo. The degree of their concern is also reflected in the law code of 1742, which directed that the penalty for unauthorized possession of a firearm within five miles of Edo's boundaries be exile.

A list given in *Edo Jidai no Hachijo-jima* (Edo-Period Hachijo Island) itemizes the crimes of the prisoners sent there in the second quarter of the nineteenth century:

DATES	MURDER	ROBBERY	FRAUD	BRAWLING	ARSON	JAILBREAK	GAMBLING	RAPE	OTHER	TOTAL
1823–40	5	2	5	13	11	14	55	19	21	145
1841–51	0	2	5	12	12	2	82	47	40	202

It is interesting that no political or ideological crimes are listed, and that some crimes (i.e., fraud, robbery, and jailbreak) are not mentioned in the law code of 1742. Crimes of a political nature did increase during this period, the beginning of the decline of the Tokugawa shogunate, and their absence here suggests that the government was dealing with these prisoners differently now or had perhaps decided (possibly because it did not want the increase made public knowledge) not to list them.

Whether they were forewarned or not, the unsophisticated islanders of the early seventeen hundreds must have been at pains to know how to deal with the new class of exiles. We can be sure at least that they didn't rejoice at the news. But what to do? *Akirameru*, resign yourself. It can't be helped. The early exiles had built up a huge backlog of goodwill and since the government made no changes in the rules for the treatment of prisoners, it was useless for simple fishermen or peasants to try to change things. Besides if the government had wanted the new exiles treated differently it would have said so. They were never lax in that respect. So the crooks and brawlers and misfits moved smoothly into Hachijo society. It was not so bad as they very likely imagined it would be. Once on the island, no one threw them into damp windowless cells or chained them to walls. They weren't suspended upside down or forced to sit crosslegged with great weights in their laps. And no one beat them with bamboo rods, branded them, stretched them on the rack, or castrated them. The new exiles did have to scratch out a living for themselves, but even the difficulties of that were ameliorated by the help of the *mizukumi-onna*. Things could have been much worse.

Criminals sentenced to Hachijo were kept in prison until the day of their departure. Once a date for departure was announced, relatives living in Edo were notified and allowed to bring the prisoners certain gifts, including things like rice and wheat, money, umbrellas, wooden clogs, and smoking pipes, all in strictly limited quantities. Items convicts were forbidden to receive were weapons and cutlery, fire-making implements, and, curiously, books. Prisoners who did not have any money were given a small allowance, the amount depending on their rank, and all prisoners were permitted to make some small purchases before leaving.

On departure day minus one the overseer would spread a straw mat in front of the jail. The prisoners would then be brought out in wrist chains and, bound together in a line with a rope tied around their waists, they would be taken for haircuts at a local barber's. When they returned they were made to sit on the mat below the prison warden, the turnkey, and a doctor. At this ceremony they were given a formal sentence, an announcement of the next day's sailing, an assignment to one of the islands of exile, and the goods sent by their relatives or their allowance of money. The medicines and ointments they had been allowed to use in jail were replenished at this time too.

The next morning the prisoners were again brought out of the jail, and this time loaded into palanquins according to their status, members of the warrior class and priests in one kind, commoners in another. This kind of segregation was extended to the methods of tying up and even to executing a prisoner. The rigidly heirarchical system pervaded all aspects of society. The prisoners were examined once more and then taken to the rear gate of the compound, where they were turned over to a representative of the assistant magistrate of Izu. From there they were taken to be loaded onto boats at Eitai-bashi, Mannen-bashi, or Reigan-jima. The boats sailed to Shinagawa, in the southeastern part of Edo, and there they waited offshore for a favorable wind to carry them to a jail at Uraga, where they were again inspected. From Uraga the prison transports headed for Miyake Island, touching at Nii and Shikine islands on the journey. The prisoners were then taken into custody by the magistrate of Miyake, and under his command they waited for the ship that would carry them on the final leg of their journey to Hachijo.

Each year only two boats transported exiles from Edo to Hachijo, one in the

44

spring and the other in the fall. Surviving records indicate no good reason why, but prisoners always were made to disembark at Miyake and there wait six months or so for the next boat. Whatever the reason, the practice resulted in great hardships for the Hachijo-bound exiles. Probably because the Miyake officials didn't want to bother with the matter, responsibility for the Hachijo exiles was given to Miyake's exiles. For a prisoner with a con man's instincts and experience this was a profitable set-up. The Hachijo exiles were like bewildered lambs, fleeced at every turn.

Waiting for them at the docks were Miyake's chief exile and his henchmen. The new men had all been in custody long enough that when someone who acted as though he were an authority gave an order they immediately followed it. It was a made-to-order situation for the Miyake exiles. Usually before the next boat came they had systematically cheated the new men out of all their money and belongings.

A petition submitted to the officials of Hachijo in 1781 by nine exiles outlines the fleecing operation. The Miyake exile chief met them immediately on their arrival and offered the ehlp of his men to carry their baggage. When they arrived at the temple where they were to be quartered, the Miyake men demanded and got exorbitant prices for carrying the goods. This was the first shakedown. The newcomers were then allowed to rest at a temple for a few days while billeting assignments were being made for them. When they were ready to leave for their new quarters they were made to pay a very large sum for lodging and meals at the temple. Their baggage was carried to their assigned villages and again money was demanded for transportation services. The exploitation continued until the newcomer was drained of all he had or until he learned to outwit the Miyake exiles, possibly even helping to fleece members of his own group. Gullible or weak men lost everything and were forced to survive through door-to-door beggary.

It is hard to believe that the officials of Miyake did not know what was going on. If there were corrupt men among them, they no doubt were getting their share of the goods. Since the Hachijo exiles were in their hands for only a half year or so, it is probable that the officials were indifferent to their problems. As nowadays, a prisoner could count himself lucky if he only had to face indifference.

When the exiles arrived at Hachijo, they were mustered on the beach before the local officials, their assistants, and the heads of the island's five villages. These men took charge of the prisoners and distributed them by the drawing of lots among the villages. The exiles then became the responsibility of gonin-gumi, five-man groups of farmers. Within a few days after his arrival, a prisoner was summoned to the home of the leader of his *gonin-gumi*. At this meeting he was instructed in the rules and regulations of the island, questioned about what kind of work he could best be assigned to, and given a general explanation of the island. Before the meeting ended, the prisoner was made to put his mark on a statement of charges that had been made against him.

An exile's five-man group helped him build a nine-by-twelve-foot hut by digging a square hole in the earth, planting pillars in it, and setting a roof on top. If the exiles cooperated in the everyday work of the farmers, they were guaranteed at least a minimal subsistence, so it was only in case of illness or when famine struck the island that they suffered severe hardships. Although exiles were under the authority of the five-man groups, they could make their livelihood by whatever means they chose. Some settled into farmwork. Those who had some schooling taught subjects such as reading, writing, and use of the abacus. The more talented of the educated exiles sometimes served as official scribes or as secretaries in the villages. (The practice of appointing exiles to official posts was forbidden in 1838, but the prohibition was never observed.) Men with the necessary skills worked as carpenters, plasterers, finishers, masons, roofers, and even as doctors. Other exiles worked as laborers on public works or at building the peculiar stone walls that enclose many island homes. The drifters who couldn't put down roots or had no roots to put down became peddlers or took up other itinerant work, traveling round and round the island like spirits in search of a final resting place. Within the confines of the island and the need to keep body and soul together, the life of an exile was relatively free.

Before the coming of the first exiles, Hachijo had been governed by Hojo So'un and before that by the Uesugi family. During this time the culture of the mainland trickled in so that what the exiles found was not a remote island totally devoid of Japanese culture but a locale somewhat backward. The exiles did, however, con-tribute greatly to the pace of cultural change that took place during the Edo period. Among introductions attributed to the exiles are broad-bean cultivation, barbering, sculpting in stone, and the manufacture of wooden clogs, palanquins, sweet-potato liquor (*shochu*), bean curds, and preserved sweet potatoes. The records mention only these but obviously this list merely begins to touch on the techniques and knowledge the exiles imported.

Most exiles cooperated with the islanders, exchanged goods with them, taught them, or worked for them. The islanders treated them kindly, taking special care of the men they respected as teachers and cultural innovators. The positions enjoyed by some of the exiles were such that they did not have to work for themselves. Their needs were taken care of by the people of their village. Until 1737, in order for them to maintain class dignity, former samurai were even permitted to wear the two swords emblematic of their rank. The practice was discontinued after that year because swords were used in an attempt to seize the deputy-magistrate's office. This was a harsh blow to the pride of the samurais, but it had to be endured and they were nothing if not enduring men.

5 ESCAPES AND ESCAPEES

HOWEVER WELL AN exile fitted in Hachijo's peculiar world, to him exile meant punishment, disgrace, and confinement. More than one exile, between bouts of resignation and despair, dreamed of escape to the mainland. Some only dreamed; some merely plotted. Some tried and failed; others made the dangerous sea journey, only to be recaptured on the mainland. A rare few seem to have reached the mainland and were never heard from again. The records say that between 1721 and 1783 there were seventeen attempted escapes, but this is misleading since successful escapes are not mentioned. This omission is partly due to the fact that when the escapees or traces of them could not be found after they left the island, there was no way of knowing whether they died at sea or on some other island. In all, approximately eighty exiles tried to escape and failed. The price of failure was death, a high risk for all but the most desperate.

In spite of the relatively good conditions on the island, the reasons for an exile wanting to escape would fill a long list. The most compelling of these is the matter of sentencing and pardons. Incredible as it seems, the exiles were never informed of the duration of their sentences: they did not know if they would be free in a month, a year, twenty years, or never. Like some of its laws, the government decided that its sentencing policy was better kept secret from all but its high officials. This system of course meant that an exile was made to wait in frustrated anticipation for a day that might never come.

A general policy of sentencing did exist. When, in 1817, a samurai named Saito Kin'ichiro was told that he was to be banished to Hachijo, he decided not to take his ten-year-old son with him, although he had been given permission to do so. The daimyo of Hida heard of the matter and admonished Kin'ichiro, warning him that he would be hurting himself if he didn't change his mind. The government's policy, said the daimyo, according to cases I've heard of, is that an exile is not to be pardoned until after five years for a commoner and thirty years for a samurai. However, if a samurai is accompanied by his son while in exile, and if the son performs his filial duties well, the term of the father's exile can be shortened by as much as ten years. Moreover, if your son goes with you and does well, he may be permitted to inherit your name and former status. The Council of Elders, in allowing you to take your son with you to Hachijo, has been generous to you. I advise you not to spurn their generosity.

Kin'ichiro followed the daimyo's advice. His son went with him and, some years later, became secretary of the deputy-magistrate's office, an honored position. Kin'ichiro was pardoned in twenty-five-years' time and father and son traveled together to the mainland where the son was made a government official.

Kin'ichiro's was an unusual case, of course. Almost without exception, the exiles marked time, never knowing if a "pardon flower," the term they used, would come in their name. The frustrations this barbarous system wrought must have been a major cause of many escape attempts.

In times of food shortages and actual famine the need to get away was simple and direct, although then few of the exiles would have had the strength or could get hold of the store of provisions necessary for the journey. There were prisoners who owed blood debts and could not rest until they had taken vengeance. There were others who had been unjustly convicted or whose punishment was vastly disproportionate to their crime. In 1747, for instance, a monk named Jiun arrived protesting his innocence. His protests continued for five years, cut off by his final protest, a fast to the death. Incredible as it seems, a man named Yamamoto Hyosuke was exiled for failure to prevent the killing of a swallow. Hyosuke had been a witness to the crime. The men who did the killing, a father and son, were put to death. The senselessness of this judgment reflects the unbalanced mentality of Tsunayoshi, the shogun who ordered the punishments. He had been told that he was unable to produce an heir because he had taken life in a previous existence, and he was advised to pay special attention to the welfare of animals. In 1687 he issued orders protecting all animals. Because Tsunayoshi was born in the Year of the Dog, he had special shelters built for stray dogs, one of which held 50,000 dogs during a two-year period. Tsunayoshi subsequently became known as the Dog Shogun.

Although he had good reason for wanting to, Hyosuke did not try to escape. He was pardoned after ten years of exile, when he returned to the mainland. Perhaps Hyosuke never tried because he never recovered from the shock of his arrest and punishment. Other exiles, with less reason but more daring, did try to break out. One of the most interesting escape stories concerns Kacho, a prostitute from Edo's Shin Yoshiwara whorehouse district, and Sawara no Kisaburo, an Edo gambler.

Kacho got an early start in her profession. When she arrived at Hachijo she was fourteen years old and already a trained courtesan. Edo society was harsh, harsh enough to allow a young girl to be forced into prostitution and harsher still to sentence her to exile as punishment for arson. The authorities could have been even more severe with Kacho, however; it was probably her tender age that saved her from being roasted to death, the usual punishment for arsonists. Sometimes too the authorities could act with macabre bizzareness. In one case a child convicted of arson was led out and tied to the stake where the roasting was to take place. All was in readiness. But then, at the last moment, the authorities stopped the proceedings and let their terrified victim off with only a severe application of moxibustion. As a child, Kacho too escaped the executioner, although as it turned out she was to meet him again.

Although there were other exiles on Hachijo who had been courtesans of some refinement, Kacho's youth, beauty, and accomplishments brought her immediate popularity. Doubtlessly she brought to this remote outpost more than a touch of the glitter and a full measure of the sensuality of the shogun's capital. For centuries Japanese society had been rigidly hierarchical and even licensed prostitutes were graded into numerous ranks, ranging from the *tayu,* professional entertainers whose elegance and accomplishments were of a high level and whose upkeep could bankrupt a prosperous merchant in no time, to the lowest of the four levels of *mise-joro,* who might or might not be able to sing, dance, or play a musical instrument, and whose services could be had for a paltry sum. Whatever rank Kacho had held in Edo, and the records are irritatingly deficient in this respect, she soon became the leading courtesan of Hachijo, a joy to the men, and the envy of her rivals.

Kacho's foremost lover, Sawara no Kisaburo, the son of a farmer from the village of Sawara, in what is now Chiba Prefecture, had received training for the Buddhist priesthood until he was twenty years old, but the lure of gambling was stronger than that of sutra chanting, burying the dead, and conducting memorial services. Gambling was a serious crime (there seems to be little that wasn't) in nineteenth-century Edo and Kisaburo was soon caught at it and banished to Hachijo. There he became a *komuso,* a flute-playing mendicant monk. He was a man of many parts and not the least of his accomplishments were a fine voice and the ability to sing the *joruri* ballads of the puppet theater. In the tiny entertainment world of the island it was not long before the suave gambler-monk and the arsonist-queen of whores met. And like the plot of a puppet drama they fell in love and soon were busy making plans to escape.

Late on an August evening in 1838, Kisaburo, Kacho, and five other exiles met in Nakanogo village. There they prepared large quantities of boiled and dried rice, two hundred dried bonitos, and filled sections of bamboo with drinking water. They carried their provisions over the mountain to Mitsune village, where they secretly boarded a small two-masted fishing vessel and set sail for the mainland.

The efficiency with which they made their plans, stocked provisions, and got off the island undetected attests to the many skills Kisaburo possessed. It appears that he also had some knowledge of seamanship and, most important for this undertaking, the tides and currents of the waters lying between Hachijo and the mainland.

By four in the morning he had the boat a long way from Hachijo. The outlook was good. No one was following them. But then, when they were between Miyake and Oshima islands, the wind suddenly changed. It blew violently, bringing black clouds and lashing rain. The crew weathered this storm, but soon after it ended a fierce wind began to blow from the south. Mountainous waves roared over the boat carrying away both masts. When it appeared that the ship might go under, the exiles cut off their hair and set it adrift in an attempt to propitiate the gods.

The boat did not sink that day. Pushed by the storm it drifted northward until, on the group's seventh day at sea, they found themselves off the coast of Hitachi, in what is now Ibaraki Prefecture. As the boat neared the shore a giant surge picked it up and sent it racing toward the rapidly approaching shore. Then, with a twisting jolt, it turned sideways and listed heavily shoreward. The exhausted escapees jumped overboard and floundered in the surf as they tried to reach the safety of the beach. Kisaburo, Kacho, and one other escapee made it, the others were swept away by the writhing surf and presumably drowned.

The survivors were helped by a man called Iwakichi, one of a group of wandering gypsy-like fishermen who roamed the coast netting fish. Iwakichi fed them gruel and fish paste and hid them until they had regained their strength. From Hitachi, Kisaburo and Kacho made their way south to Sawara, Kisaburo's birthplace, and there they were hidden by a boatman who brought Kisaburo's father to meet them. Soon they moved again, this time to Edo, where they hid themselves in the home of Kacho's parents. It was their first bad decision.

Edo was a dangerous place to be in. Government spies and officials kept a sharp lookout all the time and the appearance of strangers always drew their suspicions. Either the escapees could not get away quickly or they stretched their luck too far. After too many days had passed they finally made plans to light out for the south, to Shimonoseki, where Kisaburo's father had a trustworthy business acquaintance. They dawdled; Kisaburo paid farewell visits to friends. The days stretched out. At last it was time to go. On their last night in Edo, a farewell party was given them by Kacho's parents, a celebration the old folks would have avoided had they known it would cost their daughter her pretty head.

While the party sat toasting the fortunate escape of the lovers, the police surrounded the house. At a signal they broke down the doors, rushed in, and arrested the group. Kisaburo and Kacho had had only ninety days of freedom.

For more than two years Kacho languished in prison. Then, one day in mid-May 1841, she was led from her cell to the public execution grounds and there decapitated.

Kisaburo was luckier, although he survived Kacho by only three years. In the spring of the year that the executioner caught up with Kacho, a fire broke out in the prison where Kisaburo was chief prisoner of the East Wing. A large number of prisoners were released during the three days of the fire and its confusing aftermath. But at the end of that time all of the prisoners under Kisaburo's supervision had returned to the prison. In recognition of his services in the matter, the authorities reduced Kisaburo's sentence from execution to life imprisonment.

While in prison he wrote *Asahi Gyakuto-ki,* a journal of his stay on Hachijo, which he submitted to the prison officials. They found it interesting, and passed it on to their superiors. A number of ranking government officials who read it were deeply impressed by the author's erudition. They decided it was a shame to keep a man of such talent locked up, and in 1845 he was released on condition that he would not enter within a twenty-six-mile radius of Edo. This restriction was not enforced, possibly because the local authorities were impressed by the esteem in which Kisaburo was held by some officials of the national government. Kisaburo was dying of tuberculosis at the time of his release, and this factor too probably moved the city officials to turn a blind eye when he settled down in the Fukagawa district of the capital. His condition rapidly worsened. Within a month of his release, at the age of thirty-seven, he died, no longer an exile from the city he loved.

Before Kacho was sent to Hachijo, the prostitute most in demand had been a former Yoshiwara resident called Toyogiku. By a striking coincidence, Toyogiku had also been exiled for arson at the tender age of fourteen. Within a very short while she rose to the top of the island's professional entertainment world, a position she held for seven years. Then Kacho arrived and an inevitable rivalry sprang up. Kacho was seven years younger and fresh from Edo. She knew the latest songs and dances, the latest gossip and fashions. She was an immediate sensation. Toyogiku burned with envy. The worst of it was that everyone on the island was watching the rivals, every eye measured Kacho's rise and simultaneously noted Toyogiku's descent from popular favor. To the spectators it was an amusing spectacle and gossipy anecdotes raced wildly about the island like a grass fire in time of drought. It was as good as a seat at the kabuki or the puppet drama.

When she escaped with the island's most sophisticated, daring man, Kacho reached the pinnacle of her fame. For her part, Toyogiku could have breathed a sigh of relief, and though she would have had to endure the humiliation of knowing that she had been unmistakably bested, she could have resumed her former position with a certain measure of satisfaction.

A woman satisfied with second best would have swallowed her pride and accepted the situation. For three years it seemed to the islanders that Toyogiku was doing just that. The news of the capture of Kacho and Kisaburo trickled back to the island, and again the names of the escaped lovers were on everyone's lips. Toyogiku was extremely vexed. A few years later word reached the island of Kacho's execution, and again the stories of the rivalry were told. It was really too much for Toyogiku to endure.

If the islanders had been more aware they would have noticed a slight but significant change in Toyogiku's behavior. She began to observe closely the men she met, and to choose her clients with greater care. In the past she had selected the men who slept with her on the basis of how generous they were or, when the mood moved her, on their charm and wit, their ability to amuse. Now she searched a man's face for signs of boldness, and for the spark of discontent that could be fanned on a shared pillow to a blazing disregard for caution. She found the men she wanted, seven of them. But had she looked for other qualities—practicality, a knowledge of geography, winds, and tides, and the skill to handle a boat—she may have met a different fate.

In the third week of July 1845, Toyogiku's group gathered at midnight near the port of Kaminato. With extreme stealth they selected a boat, and when they had loaded their provisions, they untied the moorings and rowed out to sea. No one in the group had studied the local currents. Dawn found them still within sight of the island. When an early-rising fisherman found his boat missing, his fellow villagers helped him search for it. While they were looking for it, news arrived at Kaminato of the disappearance of the eight exiles. The fishermen put two and two together and sent their sharpest-eyed men to a high spot to scan the sea. They discovered a tiny speck on the horizon and decided to give chase. The fishermen knew the currents as well as Toyogiku knew the movements of her dances. When they overtook the drifting boat, they pointed their muskets at the exiles and ordered them to surrender. But the exiles had had their first taste of freedom in years. It was heady. They would probably be executed anyway. Moreover, they had heard stories of how badly the old muskets fired, especially in the hands of fishermen on a tossing sea. The knowledge made them brave. They dared the muskets and refused to give up. A former samurai among them brandished an oar like a sword and threatened to cut down anyone who attempted to board their ship. The fishermen argued with them to give up and when they met with a curt refusal they moved in as close as they dared and fired their muskets. Three of the exiles were hit and fell into the sea, where they drowned. The others quickly lay down in the bottom of the boat and begged permission to be allowed to surrender.

Whether the four other men were wounded or injured in the course of their capture is not recorded. The records simply say they died soon after. The omission is not so strange as it at first seems because it was not unusual for violent exiles to be secretly executed or for them to be helped toward a quick end by torture. Execution orders were supposed to come from the central government in Edo, but that could be a very troublesome and time-consuming process. In any case the middle-level officials did not really care how the Hachijo magistrates handled the matter. What mattered was that problems were handled efficiently and all the documents were in proper order. The death of four violent prisoners in a remote jail was easily covered over by neat-looking paperwork.

Toyogiku, however, had been the ringleader. As a lesson to the other exiles, it was decided that she should be shot. Probably the central government was not notified of this decision, for the magistrate's retribution was exceptionally swift. Sixteen days after the escape attempt Toyogiku was dragged from her cell and tied to a stake. The ordeal had deranged her mind, but she was not so mad that she forgot that only a half month ago she had been the most desirable prostitute on Hachijo. She had carefully prepared her face and wore her kimono in a voluptuous way. Then a strange thing happened. As the men of the firing squad loaded their muskets and took aim, she cried out, "Shoot! Shoot me! When I die I'll be transformed into a bug and will ruin your crops." The sound of the muskets cut off her raving. Oddly enough, the crops of Hachijo were greatly damaged that year by a plague of lady bugs. And from that time the islanders have referred to lady bugs as O-toyo *mushi*, or Toyogiku bugs.

6 THE VIOLENT EXILES

THE INCIDENT THAT has gained the most notoriety on Hachijo is called Ryuemon's Riot. It was an escape attempt, but people remember it not because anyone escaped, the exiles involved never set foot in a boat, but because it was the bloodiest of the seventeen attempts recorded.

Ryuemon's escape plans went awry before his men could even begin to carry them out. In order to assure each man that the others would not back out of the desperate enterprise, Ryuemon had drawn up a secret compact that he made everyone sign. Inexplicably, the compact was lost. A villager found it and turned it over to a magistrate who quickly alerted the heads of the five villages.

Ryuemon, who was unaware that his plans had been discovered, was captured without a fight and thrown into jail. Another plotter soon turned himself in and helped the authorities to capture three more of the group. By this time the other plotters got wind of what was up and hid themselves. There was little chance now for them to slip away in a stolen boat since all the fishermen had surely been alerted. And the escapees knew that if they gave themselves up they were sure to be punished severely; in jail they might easily die of a "sudden illness." They were desperate men and they decided to use desperate means. They needed guns and the best place to get them was Kashitate village because the security was said to be lax there. And it was. Heikichi was Kashitate's headman. He and his younger brother had received some training in swordsmanship and decided that it wouldn't be necessary to put guards on watch as the other villagers were doing. They could handle the situation.

Heikichi was awakened in the middle of the night by a loud pounding on his door. Seven exiles were waiting for him with a story about needing guns and ammunition to help put down a riot. They did not expect to be believed, and Heikichi didn't believe them, but they counted on his realizing that if he didn't give them the guns they would take them by force. Heikichi played about with them for a few minutes. He was confident that he could handle seven unarmed men. He rose and took a loaded musket from a nearby rack. He would only have to shoot one man and the rest would scurry away like frightened rats. Heikichi turned with the musket in his hands, pretending that he was going to give it to one of them. He shot the man instead. But his aim was as bad as his misplaced confidence. The wounded man drew a kitchen knife and lunged at him. In a moment the seven exiles swarmed over him with knives flashing. Heikichi never had a chance to display his skill with a sword. The knives cut into him sixty-three times before they stopped, and Heikichi lay dead in a pool of his own blood.

Before the exiles could get away, Heikichi's father and brother ran into the room. When the old man screamed at the exiles one of them thrust a knife into his mouth and killed him instantly. One of the exiles, who had lived with the family, took pity on Heikichi's younger brother and helped him to get away through a rear door. This man had a change of heart, possibly because he had not foreseen the murder of his former hosts as part of the escape plan. He decided that he wanted no part of the affair and left his fellow plotters in the house. Once outside he climbed onto the roof of the house and began banging on a metal washbasin to awaken the neighbors. The killers were outraged at his betrayal. They paid him back by dragging him off the roof and stabbing him to death.

By now most of Kashitate's villagers had been awakened, so the escapees took four guns and fled inland to Mount Mihara. The villagers discovered the three dead men and immediately formed searching parties and dispatched messengers to the other villages. The alarm spread rapidly and other searching parties were formed. At dawn one of these groups found the four guns abandoned in a yam field. Why the escapees abandoned them is a matter of conjecture. They were heavy, cumbersome things and perhaps, not knowing how to handle them properly, the men were afraid to use them. The search converged around the Mount Mihara area. A few hours later four of the escapees were surprised as they sat resting on a hillside. In their haste to get away they fell over themselves and tumbled down into the valley. The searchers quickly surrounded the area and cautiously closed in. Their caution turned out to be unnecessary: to escape the torture that awaited them in jail the rioters had cut their own throats.

The searchers left the four escapees for dead and began looking for the other two. Later the same day, when they returned for the bodies, they found only three of them: one of the men had not been dead after all and had regained consciousness and run away. He did not get very far. That evening he was found hiding in a small hut and was easily captured.

Within two days' time the seven men who committed the murders were either dead or in jail. Under torture the captured men confessed that about thirty exiles were involved in the escape plot. According to the plan, they had expected to attack homes where weapons were stored and with them seize the deputy-magistrate's office, at the same time encouraging as many exiles as possible to join their ranks. Then they planned to seize the transport boat for an escape to the mainland. Anyone, islander or exile, who stood in their way was to be killed.

The exiles who were party to the conspiracy were rounded up along with seven of their *mizukumi-onna*. Soon men began dying in the jail. One prisoner hung himself with his sash and towel. Another escaped, but when his fishing rod and towel were found on the beach, it was believed that he had drowned himself. The prisoners who did not kill themselves or die under torture were executed. In Nakanogo village they were hit with a heavy mallet that crushed their skulls. In Kashitate the men to be executed were tied to a cross and strangled to death by an exile appointed as executioner. The official records declare that all the exiles who took part in the escape plan died of illness. Probably no one believed the records, or was even expected to. And there can be little doubt that every exile on Hachijo knew what had actually happened and knew that in part at least the harsh punishments were meant as object lessons for them.

Okusuri Kinjiro, his name means Druggist Kinjiro, claimed to have run a medicine business in Edo. The records say he was a tattooed vagabond. In feudal-period Japan, just as today, tattoos were rarely worn by anyone except under-world figures or prostitutes. Whether Kinjiro had any business experience or not before coming to the island, he showed a definite knack for it once there. He built up a business and made a go of it. His methods were something else, for he was often accused of overcharging or cheating his customers. During the sixteen years he spent on Hachijo he was often in trouble and had even committed several crimes. Finally the villagers had enough of him. They protested and got the officials to send him to Utsugi village on nearby Hachijo Kojima, exiling the exile.

It was bad enough being sent to Hachijo, but to be further exiled to a tiny place like Hachijo Kojima was too much for Kinjiro to bear. Besides, his reputation preceeded him. The villagers of Utsugi wanted nothing to do with him. It would be impossible to start a new business here. Kinjiro brooded on the matter. The more he thought about it, the more he hated the islanders. In a fit of anger he decided to revenge himself on them and teach them a lesson they would never forget.

He did just that. One day in 1835, when the men of the village had gone fishing, he broke into the house of the Shinto priest. This man, who was away in Kyoto at the time, was also an official of the village. Kinjiro began his rampage by killing the priest's wife, raping two young women, and critically wounding a woman who later died of the injuries he inflicted. Then he prepared for the siege that was sure to follow. Racing about the house, he tore up all the thick straw floor mats and with them barricaded the doors. From the village chief's house he stole a bale of rice and made the rape victims cook a big pot of rice, the first he'd had in a long, long time. When he had eaten his fill, he started anew on his rampage. At the house of a man named Tsurunokyoku he smashed the furniture, tore up all the clothes he found, and threw the family's wicker storage trunks into the privy. He rode his rage like a rider on an unbroken steed. He rushed next to the house of Tsurunokyoku's brother and began to tear it apart, smashing water-storage jugs and chopping up the sliding partitions and doors. The impetus of his rage carried him on to the village chief's office, where he burned all the records, and from there he went to finish off the bridge on the only road leading from the port. He set fire to this too and, sure that it would burn down, returned to his fort to wait for the siege.

The Kojima islanders were wholly unprepared for dealing with a violent madman. When the men returned and saw what was happening, they immediately sent word to Hachijo, from which a group of men armed with ten muskets soon arrived. They avoided the burnt-out bridge by landing on the opposite side of the island and crossing over the mountain.

Inside the barricaded house Kinjiro waited, unaware that the attacking group had firearms. The Hachijo men surrounded the house and aimed their muskets at it. But their guns were useless: when the first men pulled the triggers the barrels exploded, ripping open like burst fruit. They were more dangerous to their bearers than to the target. But if the remaining muskets were useless as firearms the attackers decided they could at least be used for their psychological effect. They loaded them with blanks and fired them off, yelling and screaming all the while. Before long the attackers were surprised to see smoke rising from the barricaded house. In a matter of minutes the building was engulfed in flames. The flames leapt to the next house, and the next, and the next. Before the fire died out all the houses in Utsugi had burned down, twenty of them. In the still smoking ashes of the barricaded house they found the charred body of Kinjiro. Evidently the firing had frightened him so greatly that after setting fire to the house he had hanged himself, for the report of the incident says that "his neck was a little longer than usual."

The story of Druggist Kinjiro does not end with his death. Strangers who hear the story are surprised to learn that his grave is marked by the grandest tombstone in Utsugi. The gravestone does not indicate reverence for a man who killed two women, raped two more, and burnt down an entire village. Rather it was set up to propitiate his troublesome spirit.

Soon after World War II the fishermen's catch at Kojima decreased drastically. A sorceress whom the villagers consulted told them that the unhappy spirit of Kinjiro was casting a spell on them. She advised the fishermen to placate it by setting up a large tombstone in Kinjiro's memory. After much debate, the villagers did as she advised and, as happens in stories like this, the ruse worked, and the bonito catch of the following season was an abundant one.

7 FAMINES AND A HUNGRY GIANT

EVEN THOUGH HACHIJO held large numbers of criminals convicted for crimes of violence, incidents marked by man-made violence were uncommon there. More typical of life during the island's exile period was an endless round of demanding days in which exile and islander alike toiled to keep body and soul together. The great killers and despoilers were not the exiles but the maleficent forces of nature. The calamities that destroyed and maimed the islanders time and time again were earthquakes, typhoons and sudden squalls, disease and pestilence, failed crops, poor catches of seafood, and famine. Of these it was hunger that was most feared.

Even in good times food was not plentiful on Hachijo because of a shortage of arable land. Before the sweet potato was introduced in the middle of the eighteenth century, the people ate taros, a starchy stockroot, for their morning and noon meals and for supper a gruel of millet, barley, and vegetables. Rice was always in short supply and was eaten only by officials, priests, and by a few well-to-do families; ordinary people ate rice only at New Year's and the summer festival. Cattle were used as beasts of burden but raising livestock for consumption was anathema in Japan at this time because of the Buddhist prohibitions against eating meat. Given these precarious conditions, even slight damage to the crops was a cause for alarm. If crop damage was a local phenomenon, some help could be gotten from the mainland. But when famine was widespread, as it was in the three great famines of the Tokugawa period (Kyoho: 1732–33; Temmei: 1783–87; Tempo: 1832–36), the inhabitants of Hachijo had to rely on their own insufficient resources. The famines did not just cause hungry bellies to cry out for nourishment; they were killers. In the Tempo famine, for instance, more than eight hundred people died of starvation or related causes on Hachijo.

About midyear of 1691, the tiny island of Hachijo Kojima, which lies three miles west of Hachijo, was overrun by great numbers of rats. They multiplied profusely and in a short while ate up the island's crops. Then they began to eat weeds and the bark off trees, so that by 1692 there was nothing at all for the people to eat. Before long a few islanders died of starvation. Some food was brought from other places, but it was impossible to store on the island since the rats could not be kept from it. Early in 1693, one hundred people from Hachijo Kojima were allowed to move to Hachijo. It proved to be a temporary respite because Hachijo itself was soon suffering, first from heavy rainfalls and then from drought, so that by midsummer the Hachijoans could see the approaching specter of famine. They decided they had to look out for themselves first; it was a death sentence but they felt they had to force the smaller island's people to leave. Under duress the Kojima people returned to their homes; there was nothing else for them to do. Before the year was out all of them had died of starvation.

Within a decade famine again visited Hachijo. Fierce typhoons had raged across the island, destroying crops and sinking the fishermen's vessels. During the period 1700–01 more than six hundred people starved to death on Hachijo. Then the island was free from famine for a half-century, but in the years 1766–69 more people than ever before died of starvation. In the village of Nakanogo alone 733 of the inhabitants died, and of the entire population of Hachijo only four hundred survived the visitation.

The exiles, particularly newcomers, suffered most from the natural disasters that visited the island. Even if they had money, in time of famine there was precious little food to buy. During famines, hungry people combed the hills and the seashores for edible plants and seafood. Unknown numbers of them died from eating poisonous plants. Others in terribly weakened condition were carried out to sea and drowned while collecting seaweed and shellfish from submerged rocks. Ironically, a number of the "criminals" who succumbed to famine on Hachijo were no doubt men who had turned to crime or rebellion on the mainland as the only alternatives to starvation.

Kondo Tomizo, who was exiled to Hachijo in 1827 and pardoned in 1880, in his *Hachijo Jikki* (An Authentic Account of Hachijo) has left us a description of the famine of 1834–36, some excerpts of which follow here in a slightly condensed form:

"I was staying at the Kyuseido hall in Mitsune village at that time [1834], and on the fifteenth day of the second month [of the lunar calendar] I ate nothing but a bowl of *ashitaba* [a celery-like vegetable]. It was good.

"Around the sixth month, each morning and evening I ate soup made of potatoes and seawater, and for my noon meal I had only ground barley that had been parched. My muscles and bones became so loose that I ached all over. Early one afternoon I set out for Okago village. It took me a full half day to walk a half mile so that I did not arrive at Okago until evening. I met an exile named Kato who was very surprised to see how exhausted I was. He said to me, 'We have just finished our supper. There is none of it left. But luckily for you I've got some early sweet potatoes.' He fed me sweet potatoes that night, and the next day I was given rice and fish three times. To my surprise the condition of my muscles and bones improved right away and I was able to leave for home.

"That year the government ship did not bring us any rice or barley, only some unhulled barn grass. There was not nearly enough to meet the demand and in any case many people did not have any money to buy it with. Okuyama, the Shinto priest, gave me a bale of the barn grass, which I happily pounded in a mortar. It wasn't much but we ate it. I resigned myself to the fact that it was useless for us to even hope for anything other than sweet potatoes in the fall, even if there was a crop of rice.

"In the seventh month I stole a handful of sweet-potato leaves that had been set aside as fodder for the oxen. They made a rare dish! Not long after that I was given some sweet potatoes. They were like a gift from heaven and my joy was boundless. But I am no holy man and am rather like the ordinary people described in the proverb, 'Danger past, the gods are forgotten.' I ate the sweet potatoes and could no longer bear the thought of eating the barn grass I had once been so grateful for. Then in the tenth month, as the exquisite deliciousness of my first rice in a long time filled my mouth, I thought I could no longer eat sweet potatoes. I even complained that rice needed fish to go with it, forgetting how I had had to struggle to avoid hunger only a few days earlier. It was shameful of me to have acted in this way."

Two years later the situation was much worse, and Tomizo and his family almost starved to death. He described the situation like this: "In 1836 I decided to try my luck by going off and teaching the children of some of our wealthy families how to read. I hoped in this way to make some money for my family's needs, instead of merely staying at home and waiting for us all to die. Ukita [his wife, a descendant of Ukita Hideie] had to worry about our five-year-old daughter and two-year-old son as well as herself. She went searching for food in the mountains and down at the seashore, but because so many other people were also searching there was little to be had. Once she discovered a hill where *madami* [a tree of the camphor family] grew wild. She brought small quantities of the *madami* fruit home and pounded it into a meal for making cakes. Ukita had a malignant tumor on her breast that prevented her from nursing our son so she tried to feed him the *madami* cake, but because of its acrid smell and bitter taste he spit it out and his eyes filled with tears. Finally he became so hungry that he forced himself to eat some of the *madami* cake. Imagine the agony of this baby, and the desperate anxiety of his mother. What suffering can be compared to the helplessness of my wife as she waited for my return with only small amounts of this bitter fruit for her family!

"Soon there was not even *madami* fruit to eat, as the trees had all been picked bare. My wife then fell ill from exhaustion. My little daughter, who was afraid and helpless, wept at her mother's bedside while the baby cried constantly for want of milk. Their mother felt she had no one to rely on and must soon die. While suffering from extreme hunger, she waited for death to take her away.

"One night I returned to my family carrying only two tiny pieces of yam, each one less than three inches long. We had no place to turn for help: we were in such a pitiful state that all we could do was weep for ourselves. Even at that heaven did not forsake us. A government ship arrived at Hachijo, and through the kindness of Kameyo, wife of one of the local officials, we received a small amount of barley. We were greatly encouraged by this gift, and despite our weakness we managed to make some flour from it. The barley saved our lives."

Kondo Tomizo stands out as one of the exiles remembered by Hachijo islanders with respect and admiration. The son of Kondo Juzo, a noted explorer of Iturup Island in the Kurils, Tomizo lived on Hachijo for an even longer time than Ukita Hideie. He was exiled in 1827 and did not leave the island until 1880, when he was pardoned. By this time Hachijo had become his first home and he returned to it in 1882, remaining there till his death in 1887 at the age of eighty-two.

In spite of the respect he eventually won for himself, Tomizo came to the island with an unenviable reputation. In Edo he had been known as an arrogant and profligate young rake. Although he was the first son of a high-ranking samurai, one of those permitted to meet the shogun himself, Tomizo's tastes were not those of his class. He rejected the warrior's values of frugality and austerity and turned instead to the easy women and luxurious life of the Yoshiwara red-light district. In spite of this predilection, he was not without real talent and a taste for learning. But even in intellectual pursuits he earned the envy and enmity of many important people. He was so disrespectful of his position that his father felt it necessary to protect the family name by disowning him. That he was also an uncontrollable hothead he soon made evident.

Tomizo was living away from home in 1826 when he learned that his father was involved in a dispute with a farmer named Tsukagashi Hannosuke over land on which Juzo had built a villa. He returned to Edo immediately, convinced that it was his filial duty to settle the dispute. Inquiries he made revealed that Hannosuke was no ordinary farmer but a tough obstinate gambler who had no intention of conceding the argument simply because he was much lower on the social scale than the Kondos. When the gambler and the short-tempered young scion met there was little hope for peaceful conciliation. Almost inevitably the argument turned into a brawl in which swords and knives were drawn. Before the fight ended a lot of blood had been shed. Hannosuke the gambler had made a bad bet that day: Tomizo killed him and six members of his family.

Ordinarily when a high-ranking samurai killed a peasant he was not punished. But the Kondos had made enemies of powerful men who were looking for just such an opportunity to pull them down. Emphasizing Tomizo's generally scandalous behavior and his scorn for samurai values, his enemies were able to persuade the authorities to exile him to Hachijo. The punishment was unexpectably heavy. Perhaps as hard for Tomizo to bear was the news that his father was also to be punished. Due to Tomizo's rashness, Juzo's movements and activities were placed under such severe restrictions that he no longer could play an important part in public affairs. Two years after this disgrace, while Tomizo was in exile, the old explorer died.

The events of that year brought about an astonishing transformation in Tomizo's attitudes and behavior. Almost overnight he repented his waywardness and resolved to do a lifetime of penance. From that time forth he would take no life, not even that of a body louse. He became a model prisoner, the husband of a descendant of the noble Ukitas, the father of three children, a sculptor of Buddhist statues, and a devout Buddhist.

Tomizo was a big man, standing over six feet, and legends about his herculean strength, enormous appetite, chivalrous spirit, and selflessness have been handed down to this day. His interests and vocations were wide and varied. In addition to Buddhist statues he made miniature shrines, household furnishings, kites, and folding screens, built stone walls, painted pictures, researched and recorded the genealogies of Hachijo's leading families, wrote poetry, and worked at raising the educational level of the islanders.

Although he had been indifferent to scholarly work before his arrival at Hachijo, research and writing later became a joy to him. He became so wrapped up in it that at times it almost became an obsession. One of his poems goes: "Though determined to say no more / nor write any more, / I ink my brush—irresistibly."

Of all his many endeavors he is best remembered for writing the voluminous *Hachijo Jikki,* a sixty-nine-volume compendium of information about the island. In 1880, the Tokyo government recognized the value of at least part of this work by purchasing the twenty-nine volumes that are preserved today at the Tokyo Metropolitan Hall.

A striking omission in Tomizo's opus is any mention of violence. Never once does he mention the dramatic escape attempts, Ryuemon's Riot, murders, or executions. It is as though he had closed his eyes and ears to anything that might remind him of the cause of his banishment. Even the simple act of recording such events must have promised the torture of reliving his own misdeeds.

His aversion to killing anything, even lice, caused him ludicrous annoyances. He couldn't bring himself to scratch them so his body itched a great deal. He bore the itching as best he could but his patience was often brought to the breaking point because the lice distracted him at his favorite pastimes, writing, reading, and conversing with friends. When the itching did become too much to bear, Tomizo would grab the sleeves of his kimono and, like a man drying his back with a towel, would pull them back and forth, ever so gently, in a seesaw manner. This must have been a curious sight to see, and no doubt the children enjoyed it immensely. Their parents probably did too, although they had to save their laughter until Tomizo was out of earshot. The hard part of being his friend was that after he'd finished visiting, his host would have to rush about killing the lice Tomizo left behind.

Tomizo had an enormous appetite and an outsized body to match it. Once when he was visiting a friend, the headman of a neighboring village, he was told he could take home anything he wanted. Tomizo thanked his host profusely and asked for some rice. The bighearted headman told him to take as much as he could carry. Tomizo took him at his word. He went to the storehouse, shouldered four bales of rice, and started off for home. When the headman's helpers told him that Tomizo had walked off with three hundred pounds of rice he was flabbergasted. A hundred pounds, alright; but three hundred pounds! That was really taking advantage of a man's generosity. He couldn't ask Tomizo to return some of it, of course, but he did think he could get a large part of it back without losing face. He figured that Tomizo would never be able to carry that much weight the entire five-mile distance to his home, especially not over the mountain path he had taken. Tomizo would have to hide the rice in the mountains. The headman instructed several of his helpers to follow Tomizo without being seen. When he had hid the rice they were to wait until he was out of sight and then bring it back with them. The men quickly set off after Tomizo; it wouldn't do to let him get too far ahead because he was sure to tire soon. When, several hours later, they returned empty-handed, their master angrily asked them if Tomizo had hidden the rice before they caught up to them. Oh no, they replied, he was carrying all four bales when they first spotted him. And they had followed him right to his home because he had carried all the rice the entire distance. There is probably a certain amount of exaggeration in this tale, but it clearly indicates Tomizo's gargantuan strength and appetite.

Tomizo was pardoned on February 27, 1880. Incredible as it may seem today, he was not pardoned in the general amnesty of 1868 because of a bureaucratic error, a mistake that delayed his freedom for twelve years. Even though he had come to love Hachijo, the government's error caused him much grief, as he tells us in *Hachijo Jikki*. But, though he was an old man at the time, he survived even this blow. When at last he gained his freedom, he went to visit his relatives on the mainland, and during the two years he spent away from Hachijo, he made a pilgrimage to thirty-three Kannon temples in the western part of the country. After he returned to the island he became the head of the Obata Kannon Hall, while continuing his studies of Buddhism. Kondo Tomizo died on June 1, 1887, at the age of eighty-two, a free man and already a legend.

8 BUDDHIST IMAGES AND IMAGE MAKERS

PROMINENT AMONG THE men who introduced the mainland culture to Hachijo were the sculptors of Buddhist images. Evidence of their efforts is to be found everywhere on the island today. A walk through a cemetery or the outskirts of a village turns up literally hundreds of stone images of Jizo, Nyoirin Kannon, and many other deities. Among these weather-beaten forms are some that have been carved with surpassing skill, together with many others that are rough and artless, and still others that are unusual in one way or another. But however skillfully or artlessly made, beneath their mossy robes the images give us dim glimpses of the spirit that moved the sculptors of old.

Each image wears a unique expression. Some of them seem deep in thought, some lost in dreams. There are smiling faces too, and others clouded with anger. An uncommon few have their palms open upward while letting their arms hang listlessly, as though the artist imagined them suddenly surprised. Many people who see these statues feel an irresistible urge to reach out and caress the stone. They have that kind of appeal. Stone was not the only medium for sculpting. A look at the god shelf or Buddhist altar in an islander's home will reveal many small wooden images that are clearly the work of forgotten amateurs. There may be as many as sixteen of these in a single house. Ranging in size from over a foot tall to small enough to conceal in the hand, the images have a charm not to be found in the stone statues. They are posed in a great variety of standing and sitting postures and what is especially noteworthy about them is that they are not exact replicas of the traditional Buddhist images. In fact, they ignore the basic forms completely: the artist's response to his own inspiration is to combine in one statue Fudo and Nyorai, with perhaps a touch of the Rakan iconography. Or it leads to a surprising because unconventional depiction of the Thousand-armed Kannon bearing on his head a coiled snake. These statues have prompted such descriptions as wild and free, fearless and daring, or ignorant and primitive, but whatever the aesthetic value accorded them, they are to be found only on Hachijo.

Nature must have seemed a huge and heartless thing to many of the men condemned as criminals to Hachijo. The wonder that surrounds the images they made is that in a situation where living itself was a precarious, tenuous, and unrelieved struggle, the exiles did make them—they stole precious time and summoned up the energy to hew them from stone or carve them from wood. Sometimes they made the statues so as to earn enough money to pay for a handful of rice. And surely other images were painfully chipped out as an escape from the anguish and grief of the exile existence. That is why the Thousand-armed Kannon carries a snake on his head and why Nyorai and Rakan are joined: the tumult of grief and yearning that wracked these men is revealed in the fantastic forms they created.

People familiar only with works designed for popular taste are apt to overlook the deep strength, beauty, and emotion of these images. But these are works that ought not to be evaluated from so narrow a viewpoint. It was not so long ago that the sculpture of the ascetic priests Mokujiki Shonin (1718–1810) and Enku (?–1695) became popular. It took a very long time for people to recognize the intensity and beauty that characterizes it. This, I feel certain, will be the case with the Buddhist sculpture of Hachijo.

The Hachijo images have none of the sharpness, detail, or symmetry that characterizes the work of Kamakura-period sculptors, or that of Mokujiki and Enku. And it is possible that they represent no more than the range of vital defects in carving. Viewed differently, however, they live by the pulsing of laughter, anger, sadness, and joys that beats within them, responding to the ebb and swell of a mysterious life force unique to this island. This life force is the source of their irreplaceable charm.

In 1698 the Edo sculptor and painter Mimbu was sentenced to twelve years of banishment on Hachijo for having helped produce playing cards decorated with satirical caricatures of Tsunayoshi, the Dog Shogun. Mimbu's skill was such that he called himself a descendant of the great Kamakura sculptor Unkei and left behind on Hachijo hundreds of Buddhist images and other statues. Several excellent examples of his work have been designated as cultural properties of the Metropolitan District of Tokyo.

Before his banishment Mimbu had earned the reputation of being an entertainer on a large scale. The banquets he gave were attended by large numbers of influential men, and through his acquaintance with them he was invited to participate in the construction of the huge mausoleum being built at Nikko to hold the remains of Tokugawa Ieyasu. While Mimbu was engaged in this work he became

70

73   74

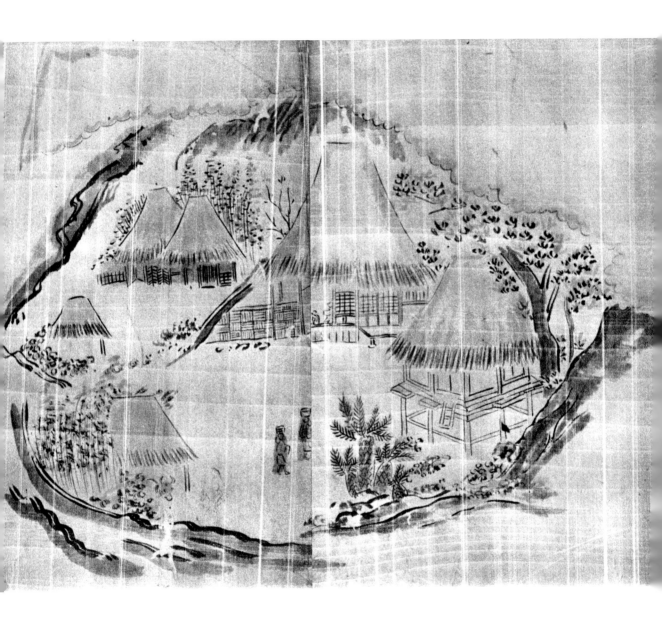

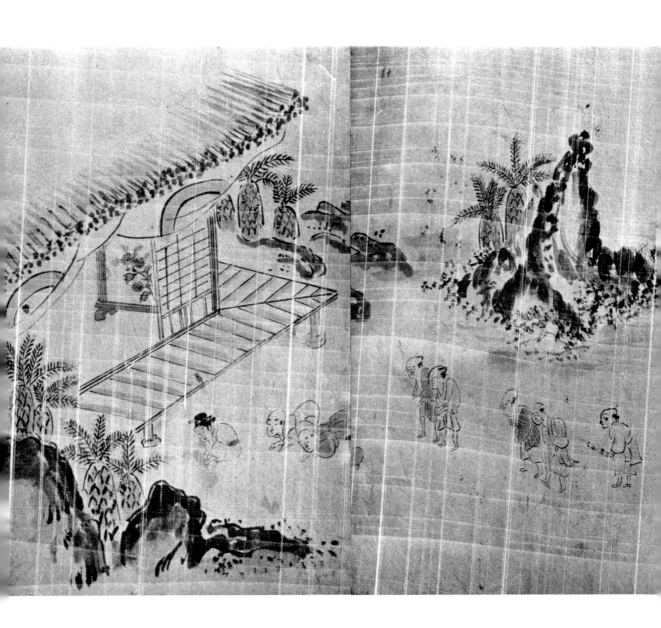

78

84

86

87

90

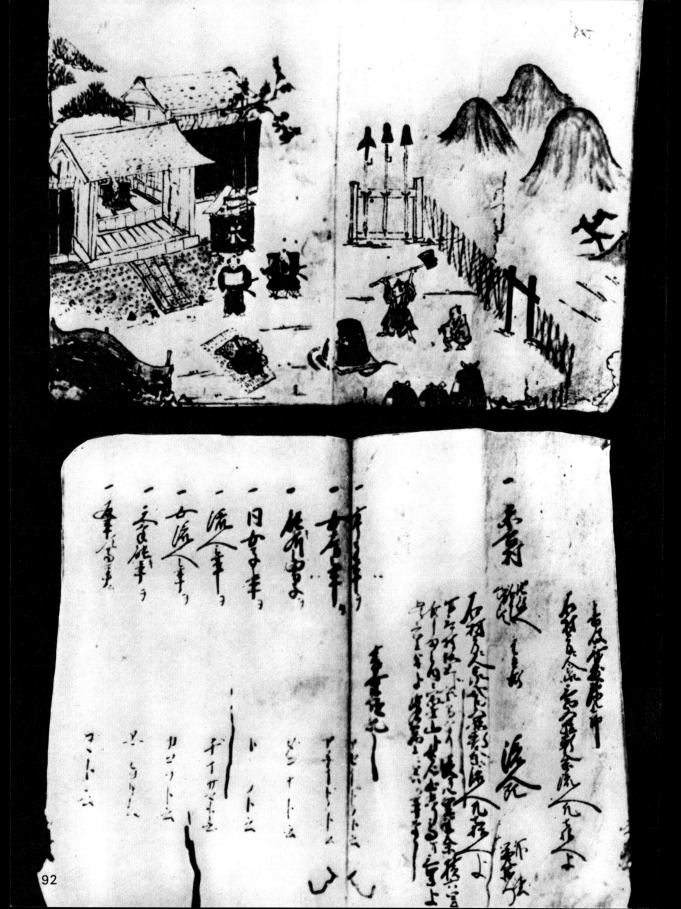

92

involved in a dispute with one of the workmen and killed him. This murder seems to have been of less consequence to the authorities than the satirization, years later, of the Dog Shogun, for in the earlier case Mimbu's punishment was merely banishment from the city of Edo.

A description that survives of Mimbu is unflattering. Pockmarked, thin, swarthy, and with prominent cheekbones, he had little to offer in the way of physical charm. But he wasn't a man to be kept down. Mimbu was an energetic, vivacious extrovert who needed adulation, and because he was an excellent story-teller with a large repertoire of amusing stories, he made himself attractive to others. Today he is remembered as a happy raconteur.

Exile meant being cut off from the novelties and luxuries of Edo that he loved so dearly, but Mimbu wasn't one to sit around brooding. He made the best of the exile situation. He got to work sculpting again even before his arrival on Hachijo, carving a statue of Yakushi Nyorai, the Buddha of Healing, while on Miyake Island. Mimbu had no inclination for anonymity, nor was he unsure of his gifts. The inscription on this work boldly states, "Made on the twenty-third day of the second month in 1699 by the great Buddha sculptor Mimbu, twenty-fifth in the line of Unkei, at the age of forty-two."

Once on Hachijo he quickly found a compatible *mizukumi-onna,* who was to bear him three sons and a daughter during his exile. He considered this alliance permanent, and when he left the island he took with him not only his own family, but also his wife's younger brother and his wife.

Mimbu was a prodigious artist, claiming to have made at least five hundred Buddhist images during his twelve years of exile. The boast may be truthful, but it is best to keep in mind his reputation as a storyteller when considering it. A number of the images he carved in 1705 (photos 82, 90, 91) are in the possession of Sofuku-ji, a Buddhist temple located in the center of Hachijo.

One statue by Mimbu has a hectic history behind it. He made it to represent Ukita Hideie, and at first it was enshrined in Sofuku-ji. A century passed and people forgot who the statue represented. The temple authorities studied the problem, and after much deliberation, decided it represented a forgotten monk of the illegal Fuju Fuse sect. Since Sofuku-ji is a Pure Land sect temple they got rid of the statue by giving it to an exile who had expressed admiration for it. When this man was pardoned, he passed it on to a Nichiren sect monk, and when the monk died sixteen years later it was inherited by Nichiju, a monk of the same sect. Nichiju thought he was getting a statue of Nichiren. He had the statue for ten years—paying it the reverence due the founder of his sect—before he chanced to discover a hollow compartment in the bottom. Inside he found poems by Hideie, his son, and grandson, as well as Hideie's autograph, and other Ukita documents. When he got over the shock, he decided the statue wasn't Nichiren after all; it most likely was Hideie. He took the statue to the head of the Ukita family and reported his discovery. There he met with another shock. Ukita doubted it really was his illustrious ancestor, and even refused the offer of the statue. Nichiju was nonplussed. Eventually, however, he did get a ninth-genera-tion descendant of Hideie's second son to accept the statue. Its identity ascer-tained, the statue remains today a possession of the Ukitas, of whom some families still live on Hachijo.

9 MYTHS, A MYTHMAKER, AND A CULTURE HERO

THE PUNISHMENT LAID on Mimbu reveals the Tokugawa government's unwillingness to allow even well-connected citizens to make light of the nation's leaders. The regime had been founded by soldiers, and though the Tokugawa men fought no wars after 1615 and the samurai had become administrators, the leaders still thought of themselves as military men. As such they had a built-in hypersensitivity to any criticism that seemed to imply a lack of martial virtue on their or their predecessors' part. Time did little to decrease this sensitivity. More than a hundred years after Mimbu was hastily packed off to Hachijo, a streetcorner entertainer, a storyteller called Tani Hidehiro, was hastened along the same route because a story he told displeased the authorities. Hidehiro told historical war stories, the blood and guts, carve-them-into-mincemeat tales which, if well told, could always be counted on to draw a crowd around the storyteller's booth.

The scanty records that survive do not paint Hidehiro as a political ideologue; in fact, he appears to have been an easygoing man who loved a good practical joke. Since revolutionaries and political firebrands are rarely—perhaps never—practical jokers, it may well be that Hidehiro's crime was simply to be carried away by his own storytelling gifts. He may have heedlessly embroidered a tale for the sheer fun of it, or to expand with laughter the shriveled generosity of a glum crowd.

Whatever offensive story he concocted (naturally the authorities did not record it for posterity), he was made to pay dearly for telling it. He was banished to Hachijo in 1810 and died there, still an exile, twenty-nine years later. Anyone would think a penalty this severe would teach a man to keep a tight rein on his tongue. Not so Hidehiro. He was irrepressible. Sometime after he arrived on Hachijo, he was approached by Ryo'on the abbot of Sofuku-ji, for help in collecting information about Minamoto no Tametomo, the celebrated twelfth-century warrior who had once controlled the Seven Islands of Izu. Hidehiro and Ryo'on, who was also very fond of martial tales, gathered together all the local folklore about Tametomo they could find. It was interesting stuff—but not quite interesting enough. No doubt there was more than a little legend mixed with the accounts they received, but that was of little consequence to men experienced in creating legendary tales. Still, it wasn't good enough.

The man the material was gathered for—through the mediation of the well-known playwright Shikitei Samba—was Takizawa Bakin, the leading literary figure of the first half of the nineteenth century. Bakin was at this time engaged in writing a thirty-volume biography of Tametomo, *Chinsetsu Yumiharizuki,* a work that was to play an important part in hallowing the warrior hero's name.

The material they collected was to Hidehiro and Ryo'on unrefined ore. Like high-grade ore it required refining, the kind of treatment a master craftsman could give it. The master craftsman in this case did not resist the temptation. He, with helpful suggestions from the abbot, worked the material over, omitting a little here, adding a little there, toning down one passage, highlighting another. Naturally, for the sake of effect, they exaggerated a bit. It was hard work, but it was fun too. When the storytellers were finished, the vague ties between Tametomo and Hachijo had been strengthened. In fact, in their account he became the founder of the Sofuku-ji temple, and the ancestor of the temple's priests.

Bakin was overjoyed at getting the stories. Probably he was used to receiving very rough-hewn information from his researchers, so that, serendipitously, the polished work that came from the Hachijo storytellers must have gratified his writer's sense of fitness. One of the genres Bakin excelled in was the didactic tale, stories in which he sought to encourage virtue and chastise vice. Probably he wished he could suitably reward the virtue of the two researchers on Hachijo, for with their help he was able to complete the monumental biography on Tametomo. Had he known the truth, however, he would probably have wished that Hachijo was a lot more remote and that storytelling exiles and priests would be banished far, far beyond the reach of hardworking authors.

One of the legends that gained acceptance as fact after it appeared in *Chinsetsu Yumiharizuki,* concerns the old belief that Hachijo was once occupied by women only. It is interesting that, whether the belief is true or not, in recorded history the female population of Hachijo has never been less than that of the male. This seems to be the reason why the island was once called Nyogogashima, or Island Protected by Women. The legend in which this idea appears concerns the first Chin emperor's search for the elixir of life. The man he chose as imperial explorer was Hsu Fu, his physician. This intrepid man sailed from China eastward into the unknown waters of the Japanese archipelago. He never found the elixir, but it seems that he did find Hachijo. During his long search, which, incidentally, ended in his death in what is presently Wakayama Prefecture, Hsu Fu's party incurred the wrath of the god of the sea. Brave though Hsu Fu was, he was very much afraid of the curse of this god, and as a propitiatory gesture he sent to Hachijo a boat containing 500 of the maidens he had brought with him. To the nearby island of Aogashima he sent another boat with 500 young men. The legend does not satisfy our curiosity as to why it was necessary to separate men and women in this way. Fortunately, the separation was not complete, and each year the men of Aogashima paid a visit to the women of Hachijo. The words of "Shome Bushi," an old folksong—"It's the south wind. / Come on, everyone, / Let's make red thongs / For the welcoming sandals"—refer to the custom of welcoming the visiting males. It seems that when the south wind began blowing around May of each year, the women of Hachijo would turn devotedly to making straw sandals with red thongs. These they set out on the beach, and then they anxiously watched for the arrival of the Aogashima men. A man stepped from his ship and put on the sandals that took his fancy. With this gesture he became the husband of the woman who had woven them; at least he was her husband until September when the wind began to blow from the north and the men sailed away to a well-deserved rest, taking with them the male children born in the previous year.

One of the more interesting details of this arrangement is its sex-lottery aspect. Granted the islanders were a superstitious people, but they were at least ingenious enough to devise a scheme for avoiding extremely chaotic, even dangerous welcomings. The arrangement also made life more zestful, since only by searching carefully would a man find sandals made by the same woman each year. Variety was easily come by. A woman who did not want to be found by last year's mate had only to alter her design. And the man who desired a change had only to avoid the too familiar woven-straw pattern. If the system did not promote stable relationships, it at least made for interesting ones.

According to Bakin's account, when Tametomo arrived in those waters, he found the men and women still living on separate islands. The situation greatly surprised him, and he, a modern man from an "advanced" civilization, scoffed at the belief that the god of the sea would punish the people if men and women lived together all year round. Like most colonizers, Tametomo had firm ideas about how civilized society should be organized and he decided to bring the men and women together. Fortunately, he didn't just run around ranting and giving unpopular orders. Instead, he set an example by taking a wife who bore him two sons while they lived together on Hachijo. When the islanders saw that there was no response from the god of the sea, Tametomo was able to transport men to Hachijo and women to Aogashima without difficulty, although surely there was some grumbling. In this way, Bakin tells us, the custom of the sexes living separately disappeared.

In gratitude to Tametomo, who was also known as Hachiro, the story continues, the Island Protected by Women was renamed Hachijo-jima, "Hachiro" being contracted first to "Hatcho" and then to "Hachijo" in the island dialect.

The island has also, at different times, been called Nyoninto and Okinoshima, and another account of Tametomo's adventures gives another version of how Hachijo got its name. According to this story, Tametomo killed a huge snake which he then cut into eight pieces, each one of which was one *jo* long—thus "Hachijo." Yet another account has it that because the island's Mount Mihara has many peaks it was called Yatake, and when Chinese characters were adopted for writing the name, these could be read either "Yatake" or "Hachijo"; in time the latter reading prevailed.

A sounder if less exotic view of how the island got its name is found in the historian Moto'ori Norinaga's book *Tamakatsuma*. There he says: "The name of the island seems to have come from the island's silk." This is backed up by an old local geography text, *Owari no Kuni Chimei Ko,* which tells us that "Hachijo Island, off the coast of Izu, probably came to be so called because *hachijo* [eighty-foot] cloth was produced there." These accounts support the view that during the Muromachi period, the mid-fourteenth to mid-sixteenth century, when the *kihachijo* silk produced on the island was sent to the mainland as tribute, it became the custom to call the island by the name of its product.

As a scholar, our revisionist historian Tani Hidehiro may have been aware of the more prosaic accounts of the origin of the island's name. As a storyteller, however, he was more interested in a good tale than in any dry-as-dust historical "facts." No doubt he would have agreed with Anatole France, who many years later remarked, "When a history book contains no lies it is always tedious."

Hidehiro was surely one of the "men of culture" whom the islanders welcomed. But even more welcome than the playful storyteller was Tanso Sho'emon, the man who taught the islanders to make sweet-potato liquor. Because Hachijo had so little land suitable for rice cultivation, the islanders were prohibited from brewing sakè, Japan's traditional alcoholic drink. The prohibition was felt to be unjust and was ignored wherever possible. But the scarcity of rice and its exceedingly high price caused sakè to be a luxury denied most islanders and exiles.

Before his imprisonment Sho'emon had been a trusted official, a shipping agent of the Satsuma daimyo, a job at which he developed rich tastes. So when he arrived on Hachijo to begin what was to be a fifteen-year sentence for smuggling, he decided that banishment without alcohol was intolerable. He set about at once to improve the situation. At first he tried using locally grown sweet potatoes. These produced poor results. At home in Satsuma, Sho'emon had tasted good sweet-potato liquor, so, efficient businessman that he was, he sent off to Satsuma for sweet potatoes and alcohol-making equipment. The supplies and equipment were a long time coming, there being only two boats a year from the mainland, but the Hachijoans had nothing if not time. At least a year must have been consumed in getting the supplies. But once they were landed Sho'emon and his anxious helpers immediately set about cutting up sweet potatoes and planting them in a fertile field specially set aside for the project. Next the new equipment was set up, ever so carefully. And with that done there was nothing to do but tend the crop and wait for nature to play her part. The crop prospered: no drought dried up the tender shoots, no typhoons washed away the nutritious soil, and no Toyogiku lady bugs ravished the delicate leaves.

A good crop is always welcome, the bounty of the gods of the earth and the sky. The gods must be thanked, of course, and in proper fashion. And what could be more suitable thanks than offerings of strong alcoholic drink. After all, the link between alcohol and religion must be as old as exile itself. Sho'emon's sweet-potato crop was doubly welcome. The sweet potatoes were harvested almost before they were ready, and immediately the Satsuma apparatus started working.

The experiment was a success. Everybody said so. And the more they tasted the fruits of Sho'emon's efforts the more they said so. It was unanimously agreed that the Satsuma sweet-potato crop would have to be doubled, at least, in the coming year. Sho'emon was a culture hero. A shrewd operator at heart, he probably capitalized on his newly won popularity.

When the Tokugawa government was replaced in 1868, the Satsuma forces were in the vanguard of the new, Meiji, government. Although Sho'emon had been gone for fifteen years, his old friends had not forgotten him. As soon as things could be worked out he was invited to return to the mainland. And to make sure everyone understood that this was not an amnesty for an ordinary criminal, he was given treatment equal to that usually accorded a ranking samurai: a party of mounted men was sent to escort him on his return to the capital. No doubt the islanders, doubly impressed by this treatment, gave Sho'emon a memorable send-off. And to this day he is remembered fondly, as sweet-potato liquor remains one of the most popular drinks of the islanders.

IO THE LAST EXILES

DURING THE SECOND half of the nineteenth century Japan was a nation in great turmoil. For most of the entire two hundred and sixty-five years of the Tokugawa shogunate the nation had kept itself free of foreign intrusion. A few Dutch and Chinese traders had been permitted to reside and do business on a tiny island in Nagasaki harbor, but their influence had been severely restricted. The isolation policy was a remarkable success. Until the early eighteen hundreds, that is. Then American, British, French, and Russian ships began entering Japanese waters in slowly increasing numbers. When the Japanese repulsed the foreign trading ships, warships were sent to frighten them into opening the country. The Japanese had no warships of their own and their shore batteries, as it turned out, were ridiculously ineffective against the foreigners' guns. When the Japanese leaders recognized their nation's weakness, they hastily adjusted to the circumstances. In 1856, Commodore Perry forced them to accept the American consul general Townsend Harris. Sixteen months later a trade treaty was signed by America and Japan, and with this agreement, the centuries-old barriers against foreigners were rapidly taken down.

The changes that came with the end of the national isolation policy affected all institutions. The Japanese had fallen far behind the West in many fields and needed desperately to catch up. To fail to do so would mean going the way of imperial China, which was at this time being divided into "spheres of influence" by the major Western powers. The Japanese responded rapidly—and successfully: within twenty years the shogunate was finished and a new government, determined to discard the feudal system and modernize the nation, had taken control of the country. Astonishing reforms were carried out in a remarkably short time, and the birth of a modern nation was under way.

In 1868 Edo was renamed Tokyo, "the Eastern Capital," a constitution was promulgated, and new organs for administering the country were established. In the following year the feudal provinces were designated prefectures and the feudal lords governors. Drastic reforms were carried out in all areas, with not one of the feudal institutions left untouched. The reforms made in the area of law were particularly far-reaching. In 1868 a report on the investigation of the shogunate's trial records suggested that crucifixion be reserved as punishment only for high treason, that roasting to death be abolished, and that exile be limited to Hokkaido. Torture of prisoners, a technique commonly used for extracting confessions, was also abolished, and laws, which once had been secret, were now published so that anyone could know them. New laws were promulgated in 1870, 1871, 1873, and 1880, the latter ones based chiefly on French models. These laws heralded the abolition of feudalism and the end of the traditional class system. From this time on the emphasis was to be on legal rights rather than on social obligations, although it would take a long time for the concept of rights to seep into the public consciousness.

In spite of the rash of changes in law and penology, it was not until 1881 that exile to Hachijo was terminated. The concepts of punishment were changing but the government still felt that exile served a purpose in providing a means of getting troublemakers out of the way during the hectic reorganization of the state.

The process of modernization was bewildering to everyone, even to those who welcomed the end of the tottering, backward-looking shogunate. To the traditionalists, who saw the confusing changes as omens of disaster, the new age was a horror to be resisted mightily. It was inevitable, then, that there would be clashes between those who looked toward the future and those who clung to the past. One of these clashes occurred in Shikoku, where the province of Awa had been designated as Tokushima Prefecture. Hachisuga, the feudal lord of Awa, accepted the changes, and in his new role as governor of the prefecture he decided to visit Tokyo in 1870. He chose a bad time to be away. Some of his men, under the leadership of the former chief retainer, decided that they would resist the new system, especially the reorganization of the political structure. Awa would remain Awa, they decided, despite the emperor's edict to the contrary.

The rebels expected opposition, and it came almost immediately under the leadership of a samurai named Ueda Jingoemon Tomoyasu. The dissension between the two factions spread and before long the entire prefecture was split into two mutually hostile camps. Ueda made a rash decision. He probably knew that in the eyes of the new government the worst thing was not resistance to the new policies—the reformers expected resistance and believed they could handle it—but armed conflict between those for and those against the policies. Once a group resorted to armed force the whole nation might fall to fighting. Nevertheless, the situation in Tokushima worsened, until finally Ueda felt he had to use force. His men attacked the chief retainer's and succeeded in repressing them. Then Ueda and his men sat back and waited for the government's reaction.

When the judgment came down it was against Ueda. Together with nine other men, the order stated, Ueda was to be banished to Hachijo. Twelve others were held responsible for the disturbance and were banished to another island. From this point the record grows spotty. Seven of the ten men dispatched to Hachijo never made it, their records noting only that they died of illness on Oshima Island while en route. Ueda himself survived to reach Hachijo, where he stayed until he was pardoned in 1873.

Although semi-isolated, Hachijo felt the tremors of change that were rocking the mainland. For a long while the mood of the exiles was one of frustrating suspense. A rumor would be born, grow to fantastic proportions and forms as it raced from prisoner to prisoner, and then it would be eclipsed by two, three, or a half-dozen other rumors. What, the exiles wanted desperately to know, was *really* happening? And how would it affect them? The political prisoners raised the highest hopes. With the downfall of the shogunate, they would no longer be enemies of the state. They might even, the optimists believed, be hailed for their opposition to the shogunate and have their lands restored and be given new titles. Even the common criminals saw a ray of hope in the sweeping changes being carried out. A new state was in the making, and what better way of heralding it than with an act of mercy, a magnanimous gesture of forgiveness for all those who had trespassed against the old—and now scorned—state?

In spite of the many misleading rumors, the fervent hopes of Hachijo's exiles were not nurtured in vain. In 1868, to commemorate the start of the Meiji (Enlightened Rule) era, a general amnesty was declared and most of the exiles were pardoned. For those men it was a joyous time. But if the islanders thought the amnesty spelled the end of Hachijo's history as a penal colony, they were mistaken, for the new government continued to banish criminals to their island until 1871 and the last exiles were not freed until ten years later.

The last exiles to leave Hachijo were seven men who had participated in an escape attempt that was foiled in 1873. It is noteworthy that, as a sign of the changing times, the thirty-six men who were a party to the escape plot were not executed, the traditional punishment.

Little else besides the names of the last exiles is known. The official records do not even mention their crimes, of so little distinction were they. These men did not remain on the island after being pardoned, as did Kondo Tomizo and several others who had been pardoned earlier. Presumably they returned to the mainland, there to fade into historical obscurity. Among those who did stay on was a man named Tokujiro, a pickpocket from Tokyo. After gaining his freedom, Tokujiro decided to make Hachijo his home. He stayed on the island, a living monument to the island's unsavory past, until his death in 1926.

MORE THAN EIGHTY years have passed since Hachijo's last exile received his pardon flower, eight decades that have seen Japan transformed from a backward nation acutely conscious of her new international identity to the world's second greatest economic power. Hachijo has also changed considerably, but while the nation as a whole continues to hurtle into the future, life on Hachijo moves forward at a far slower pace, as though the islanders were unwillingly being dragged away from the island's storied past.

But there is no stopping the headlong rush. In the late 1960s entrepreneurs awoke to the island's potential value in the "leisure boom" that was and still is sweeping over the nation. So now Hachijo is rapidly becoming a resort area for the tens of thousands of Japanese avid for travel and recreation in unfamiliar surroundings. Planeloads of tourists fly in from Tokyo seven to ten times a day and in summer tourist-burdened ferries call at the island's ports every day. The new money is already transforming the island, turning the eyes of the young to the bright new future revealed in the color-TV commercials.

The incoming planes and boats bring no prisoners these days as the only jails are the police lockups that hold prisoners temporarily. Reversing the old process, convicted criminals are now sent to prisons on the mainland, although fortunately there are few prisoners to send away. The exile period is now so far in the past that there is no shame attached to having an exile for an ancestor. In fact, having one adds a little zestful color to the family tree, for the exiles are a vibrant part of Hachijo's living history.

LIST OF CAPTIONS

Color Photographs

A. Moonlight on the sea surrounding Hachijo.

B. A map of Hachijo made by Kondo Tomizo, an exile who spent fifty-eight years on the island. It is not known how Tomizo made his measurements but they are surprisingly accurate. The date Kyoka 3 (1846) is given at bottom left. Collection of Takeo Nagatoro, Sueyoshi, Hachijo.

C. Hibiscus and betel-nut palm, among numerous other plants, are typical of the island's vegetation.

D. Azaleas and a cobblestone wall. The stones are carried from the seashore where the waves have worn them smooth.

E. Chamomiles in bloom before a thatch-roofed storehouse.

F. In addition to semitropical plants, Hachijo islanders enjoy the cherry tree with its evanescent blooms.

G. In the background Mount Hachijo Fuji, a volcano that erupted in 1487, 1518, 1522, 1523, and 1707. In the foreground is a freesia nursery. The bulbs of this member of the iris family are shipped to the mainland and are a source of the island's economy.

H. In 1887, the last year of his life, Kondo Tomizo lived in this house. Built of hard alder wood, the house has resisted decay and is still used as an assembly hall.

I. A wooden Buddhist image that is believed to have been sculpted by Kondo Tomizo. Property of Taishi Hall, Nakanogo, Hachijo.

J. Statue of Amida Buddha carved in wood by Kondo Tomizo.

K. *Runin-butsu,* or exiles' Buddhist images. Many such images were sculpted by amateur craftsmen among the men banished to Hachijo. Even today the islanders lay offerings of flowers before the holy figures.

Monochrome Photographs

1. An autumn sunset on Hachijo Kojima, the tiny island that lies three miles west of Hachijo.

2. Hachijo Kojima seen from Hachijo, with Mount Hachijo Fuji at middle right.

3. *Hego,* a large fern. Hachijo is the northernmost limit of the area in which this plant grows naturally.

4. Plant life springs luxuriantly from Hachijo's rich soil. In many places the vegetation is as dense as jungle growth.

5. Yaene Port, one of many small fishing harbors built on solidified lava flows.

6. The rocky coast of Hachijo with Hachijo Kojima in the background. The tidal current between the islands is swift and dangerous.

7. Waves crashing on Hachijo's shore.

8. Hachijo Kojima seen from Yaene Port. In a fit of anger, Druggist Kinjiro killed two women and himself and burned down an entire village of twenty houses here in 1835. Since 1969 the island has been uninhabited.

9. The outer rim of Mount Hachijo Fuji's crater.

10. A cliff at Borawazawa. Hachijo's coast is marked by a number of high cliffs such as this one. The authorities sometimes executed exiles who committed serious crimes on the island by having them thrown off a high cliff.

11. Coastal road running between Okago and Yaene.

12. The wild coast of Hachijo. When famine struck, many exiles and islanders alike, weakened by prolonged hunger, were drowned while trying to gather seafood at places like this.

13. The kind of scene that greeted arriving exiles, the austerely forbidding beauty of Mount Mihara.

14. At Yaene, Mount Hachijo Fuji looms behind the graves of anonymous victims of disasters at sea.

15. Hydrangeas growing near the summit of Mount Hachijo Fuji.

16. The coast at Mitsune. The tortured look of the rocks is the result of the meeting of molten lava with the sea. Hachijo has no sandy beaches; its shores are made of pebbles, boulders, and lava.

17. A legend says these stones mark the grave of seven Buddhist monks who died here. Another says the stones stand over the grave of some exiles. On the four large stones are carved the words *Namu Amida Butsu,* "For the Mercy of Buddha Amida." One stone carries the date 1805 and another 1825.

18. *Han'ya no fune,* boat models used as offerings, are customarily placed on the graves of the victims of sea disasters. According to a spirit medium, the spirits of people who die at sea always ask for these boats. The picket-shaped stakes contain prayers for the spirits of the dead.

19. Precincts of the Mishima Shrine in the mountains of Nakanogo. The tiny stone

houses contain plaques that are objects of worship.

20. Asama Shrine. Located on top of Mount Hachijo Fuji, the shrine is represented by the large tree behind the numerous torii gates. The cobblestones, objects of worship, are carried from the coast.

21. A stone sanctuary.

22. Graves and cobblestone offerings. On Hachijo, graves are not marked with the names of the dead; instead, visitors identify a grave by the arrangement of the cobblestones placed around it.

23. In order to protect them from typhoons and windstorms many houses are protected by a cobblestone-enclosed embankment like this. The embankments are often six feet high and nine feet wide and have planted on top trees of the pasania, camellia, and camphor families. Many of these walls were built by exile laborers who were paid several small balls of cooked rice for a day's work.

24–25. The floors of these thatch-roofed storehouses are built about six feet above the earth to avoid damage by rats and dampness. Although nonperishable goods may be kept on the ground below, the actual storeroom is just under the roof.

26. Before automobiles were brought to the island, oxen such as this one were commonly used as beasts of burden. Although the islanders, as Buddhists, disliked eating meat, at times of severe famine they killed and ate oxen.

27. A specialty of Hachijo is the Tametomo kite, so called in honor of the twelfth-century warrior Minamoto no Tametomo, who once ruled over the Izu islands. The first such kite is believed to have been made by the ingenious exile Kondo Tomizo.

28. Drummers beating a Hachijo-*daiko.* At one time during the exile history of the

island samurai exiles were permitted to wear the two swords that were the symbol of their status. A legend says that when the privilege was withdrawn after an attack on a government office by exiles bearing swords, some exiles took up sticks and with them beat on the Hachijo drum to give vent to their indignation. Traditionally the drum is beaten on both sides by two women facing each other. One of them beats time while the other improvises the rhythm.

29. At festivals on the island one of the feature attractions is the rice-hulling song that is accompanied by the pounding of rice in a large wooden mortar.

30–31. Dyeing and spinning of *kihachijo* silk. The yellow silk has been a much-desired product of Hachijo for several centuries and was at one time sent as tribute to the mainland.

32. The last practitioner of her craft, Bin Tamaoki still weaves *kihachijo* sashes and straps on this primitive device.

33. An old woman of the island relaxes with a cigarette.

34. Basket-making, another of the intricate crafts of the island.

35. This potting studio is the only one on Hachijo. Shokichi Aoki, the potter shown here, uses camellia ash and lava in his glazes to produce unique effects.

36. A shipwright at work.

37. A Buddhist image dedicated to the exiles. Worshipers who invoke the god's favor customarily do so by dressing an image in a bib-like garment. It is believed that the wish will be granted only if the garment is put on in secret; consequently it is often done under cover of darkness.

38. On the mainland the dead are cremated, but on Hachijo they are buried in graves that are marked as this one is.

39. Many of the Buddhist images bear a tranquil expression similar to this one, but some of them reveal the anguish of the exile sculptors.

40–48. Buddhist images like those shown in these photographs are found all over Hachijo. The exiles sometimes sculpted them as acts of devotion and sometimes for patrons who commissioned the works, often for extremely small sums.

49. Images of Jizo, the guardian deity of children and travelers, are often placed near the graves of children in Japan. Parental love for the spirits of the deceased children is shown here by the clothing placed on the images.

50. A gravestone like this probably indicates that two children died at nearly the same time and were buried together.

51. These images are dedicated to a family's deceased parents and grandparents.

52–69. Buddhist images typical of those found scattered all over the island. Many of those made by exiles were carved with stone tools, since most exiles were not permitted to have cutting tools of any kind. Sometimes an image took an exile years to sculpt, and with this act of arduous piety the sculptor hoped at its completion to be granted a pardon.

70. A sixfold screen painted by Kondo Tomizo showing the island's rice-planting cycle from (right to left) groundbreaking and plowing to harvesting and packing the rice in straw bags.

71–72. Wooden statues of Buddhas. They are thought to have been carved by Kondo Tomizo. Height (left), 12.6 cm., (right) 14 cm. Collection of Toyo Kikuchi, Nakanogo, Hachijo.

73–75. Wooden images by anonymous sculptors. At left are two Buddhist images, at center is Ebisu, god of commerce, and at right Fudo, the Immobile One. Heights (left to right), 14 cm., 33.5 cm., 12 cm., 24 cm. Collection of Kaoru Nishizaki, Nakanogo, Hachijo.

76. A painting showing Hachijo houses of a bygone era. Collection of Hachijo Town Office.

77. A painting depicting a poor but virtuous woman being presented at the deputy-magistrate's office where she is to receive an award. According to an old tale, the woman shown here was a model of filial piety, a major virtue according to the Confucian code of ethics prevalent in Japan in the Edo period. She was highly praised for her virtue by the authorities, who held her up as an exemplar of how a daughter should behave. Collection of Hachijo Town Office.

78–79. Genre paintings of Hachijo women of the Edo period. The two women at left are shown in typical working attire while the other two are dressed in the fashion for greeting arriving and departing boats. Reprinted from *Shichito Nikki* (Seven Isles Diary).

80. A wooden image by an anonymous sculptor of Daikoku, the harvest deity. He is shown carrying a sickle and rice sheaves. Collection of Katsutoshi Yamashita, Nakanogo, Hachijo.

81. Miniature wooden image of a Buddha in a bamboo case. Height, 4 cm. Collec-

tion of Harue Kikuchi, Nakanogo, Hachijo.

82. Wooden image of Tanno Soteki, chief priest of Sofuku-ji temple, by Mimbu. Circa 1698–1709. Collection of Sofuku-ji, Okago, Hachijo.

83. Wooden image of a Buddha by an anonymous sculptor. Collection of the Kannon Hall, Mitsune, Hachijo.

84–87. Wooden friezes at Sofuku-ji temple by the exile-sculptor Kubo Chojuro. He carved these during the period 1747–54. Chojuro also painted murals on the ceiling of the temple, but these have since disappeared.

88. Wooden image of the Amida Sanzon, Amida Buddha with his Boddhisattva attendants Kannon and Seishi, by Kondo Tomizo. Collection of Motoshiro Osawa, Nakanogo, Hachijo.

89. Weather-beaten wooden image of Jizo by an anonymous sculptor. Collection of Omi Hall, Nakanogo, Hachijo.

90. Chief priest Oyo Reikan (died 1686), by Mimbu. Sofuku-ji temple. Wood.

91. Sakyamuni Buddha, by Mimbu. Sofuku-ji temple.

92. Four pages of *Asahi Gyakuto-ki*, by Sawara no Kisaburo, who made the only known successful escape from Hachijo. This book is an account of his exile on Hachijo. The illustration on the upper two pages shows the execution by beheading of an exile.

The "weathermark" identifies this book as having been planned, designed, and produced at the Tokyo offices of John Weatherhill, Inc. Book design and typography by Ronald V. Bell. Layout of photographs by Keisuke Konishi. Gravure and 4-color letterpress plates engraved and printed by Toppan Printing Co., Tokyo. Composition and printing by General Printing Co., Yokohama. Bound at the Makoto Binderies, Tokyo. Text is set in 12-pt. Perpetua Roman with hand-set Futura Light for display.